REDEFINE YOUR APPROACH TO LIFE

YOU.

SAGAR MAKWANA

NOW!

FiNGERPRINT!

Published by
FiNGERPRINT!
An imprint of Prakash Books India Pvt. Ltd.

113/A, Darya Ganj, New Delhi-110 002,
Tel: (011) 2324 7062 – 65, Fax: (011) 2324 6975
Email: info@prakashbooks.com/sales@prakashbooks.com

facebook www.facebook.com/fingerprintpublishing
twitter www.twitter.com/FingerprintP
www.fingerprintpublishing.com

Copyright © 2023 Prakash Books India Pvt. Ltd.
Copyright Text © Sagar Makwana

ISBN: 978 93 5440 736 9

Processed & printed in India

To my guru, my mentor, and my inspiration—
my father, and to his guru (Navajyothisri Karunakara
Guru) with whom he resides now.

Paa, until I join you, know that every single thing I
do is a dedication to you.

For without you, I am but an empty vessel.

Foreword

"Your visions will become clear only when you can look into your own heart. Who looks outside, dreams; who looks inside, awakes."

Carl Jung

Startled and drenched in your sweat, you wake up. What a nightmare you had. Someone was trying to disfigure your face. You freak out and try to feel your face with your hands. It seems fine but you want to *see it* to believe it. You reach the mirror inside your room but the mirror is dirty. You can't see yourself properly. Desperately, you breath on it and itbecomes foggy. And as you clean the glass with a towel, you are able to see a clearer image. Everything is fine. Nothing has happened to you. It was just a bad dream. You breathe a sigh of relief and get back to sleep.

This is an experience no one wants to have. Yet, in some ways, this experience exactly describes how we live our lives. In the nightmarish world of achieving goals, targets, and milestones, we forget who we are, what we are meant to be, and what we are capable of doing. And when we finally wake up from the nightmare, we are desperate to search for answers amidst the dirt and the fog that has blurred our life. These answers usually come from the words of wise men/women that shine like a guiding light in our path.

No, I don't consider myself to be the wise man. My humble attempt through this book is to be *the mirror* that shows you a reflection of your own life. To show you that you aren't as broken as you imagine yourself to be. To help you look beyond the assumptions that have marred your vision. To nudge you into aspiring to be a *new* you that exuberates a sense of freedom, purpose, and vigour that seems almost invincible.

For there always comes a point in life when we seem to be living someone else's life, having subconsciously or consciously imbibed their opinions. With this book, I believe you will find a path, a will, to change. You will live an authentic life, one that is completely and wholly yours. And you will finally see that you, like all humans, are full of endless possibilities, as endless as the horizon itself.

Contents

1

Killing It with First Principles Thinking

Clarity and confusion—two words that contradict each other, and yet, in tandem, capture the story of our lives. Two words that are opposites, and yet walk hand in hand to help us understand life's philosophy.

Can you remember when you were the least burdened by life's demands? For most of us, this phase would pertain to childhood. Even if we don't remember every detail of our childhood, we can't deny that those were the years when we had the least amount of worry.

Not enough money? Who cared when you had all the dirt in the world to play with and all the time to stare at the clouds in the sky. Not enough fame? Who cared when you were able to get all the love from your family, along with the attention and pampering that came from the same relatives who now annoy you. Not enough space? Who wanted all that when you could blissfully curl up as your mother gently caressed your hair. Not enough goals? Who cared when you could, without a care, run amok and break things on the way. Not enough clarity? What meaning did you need when you could spend time playing the stupidest games with your friends.

Once we reached our adolescent years though, we grew more curious about the world and its ways.

This curiosity led to clarity, but the clarity also led to confusion.

Let me explain why.

As you grow up, alongside figuring out what works in life, you also get perplexed as to why it must work that way. Someone suggests that you are brilliant and hence you should pursue science. And you wonder why you can't take up arts instead. Someone claims that you can't perform certain duties during your periods and that you should confine yourself to a room. And you wonder why this should be the case. Someone says that you can't cry because you are a boy and, apparently, boys don't cry. And you wonder if being a boy is an epitome of strength or merely a shackle you can't release yourself from. Someone says that you have certain responsibilities that you shouldn't forego. And you wonder why responsibilities are always given and not chosen.

The more we gain clarity about norms and rules, the more confusing these norms themselves become. The more the world around sets highly visible and flaunted standards to follow, the greater the gnawing sense of confusion within us becomes. As we grow up into responsibility-hoarding, goal-addicted, achievement-flaunting, envy-filled, distraction-hungry adults, we tend to forget who we are and what we want from our lives. This, my dear friends, is the irony of life and is truer today than ever. We have a complete sense of what we want to do and yet we are lost.

Like most people, you may believe that you are here to achieve something. You may not know what and you may not know how, but you have been made to feel like you are on a mission. You have been given a list of things to complete before you can breathe a sigh of relief. Do you think this will happen though? Do you believe that when you finally achieve what you want to, you will get that sense of satisfaction, happiness, and a feeling of accomplishment?

Let me share my own experience with this predicament.

I was about 20 when I first began to believe that I was on a mission. I started to focus on goals and achieve them. One milestone, and then another, and then more. I didn't stop. I didn't look back. I was focused. I landed a good job. I got married to a beautiful person inside and out. I then started my business, built an amazing team, got the business flourishing, and then started another. I made things happen by collaborating with some wonderful people. I felt that there was nothing in this world that could stop me. Even so, I kept thinking that there is so much more I haven't done yet.

Soon, however, I realized the ugly truth: my passion was being triggered by others.

It was a race. But I didn't know what I was running toward. Slowly, the goals became obscure. I realized I was running toward nothing. Life got weird at that point. I would mentally tune out of fun conversations. I would address my team as if it were a task. I stopped living in the moment and started to live in my thoughts. I missed being in the present. I still loved my wife, but sometimes I lost a sense of being truly and wholly with her.

During this period, between the ages of 28 and 31, many noteworthy incidents happened to me. I will talk about some of them as we go forward, but my biggest lesson came in January 2021.

There comes a moment in your life when all that you have been through starts to make sense. All your experiences, all your pain, all your joy, wishes, dreams, and aspirations connect to reveal something, and that moment is worth living over and over again. For me, it was the day I was introduced to First Principles Thinking (or FPT).

I was attending a session conducted at one of my business forums. A fireside chat with Suresh Sambandam, the then CEO of KissFlow, a leading cloud-based B2B Indian tech company, had been organized. While he was talking about what had influenced him the most, he happened to mention that he usually based his decisions on 'First Principles Thinking.' I didn't know what FPT was then, but I was tuned in.

After the session got over, I remember asking him this question: "Can you elaborate on First Principles Thinking and tell me where you first heard about this concept?"

He then shared some valuable snippets of information on FPT and told us that he learnt about it in a boot camp but didn't remember which one. After he finished, I thanked him and told him that I will never forget this day, because this was the day I first heard about FPT as a concept. I am etching that moment in this book forever because I feel that my life pivoted at that moment, on that day.

We will discuss FPT in this chapter in detail. In brief, it is a technique that helps people to approach issues based on core underlying principles rather than generic assumptions, and most of the assumptions we hold obscure our real needs and wants, preventing us from charting our ideal path in life.

Take a job interview, for example. "Where do you see yourself in five years?" This outdated question is still asked in interviews, where you are expected to prove that you are a self-aware, mature adult. The employer asks for countless things from you, and in return, they promise to pay you a good salary. You say yes because you have been told that having money is important, and you sign up for this contract . . . until you no longer want to be a part of it. You realize that all that you ever wanted was some amount of comfort from the money that you earned. More importantly, you wanted peace of mind, a sense of fulfilment, and lots of love. But instead of getting these, you got something else.

At one point, we can get out of this vicious cycle of confusion, of not knowing what is truly important, and that point arrives when we start removing assumptions from our lives— assumptions that our mind has been conditioned to believe since childhood.

Breaking out of the web of assumptions confers many advantages, but the most powerful among them is that it lets us realize, finally, that everything is uncertain. Right from the get-go, our whole world dwells around uncertainty. The day you are certain that something won't go wrong is the day it will. I didn't say this. Murphy did, when he coined his law:

"Anything that can go wrong will go wrong."

The right way to deal with uncertainties is by acknowledging them instead of denying they exist. According to the writer and coach Mark Manson, much of the self-help world works by denying uncertainty and peddling narratives of "your life is perfect right now as is" rather than empowering people to take stock of the current situation and face it. Many self-help gurus pep you up with rituals or activities that merely provide a temporary high. Once you believe that these exercises do work, you will seek them out more, getting caught in a vicious cycle. Remember that no happy person ever had to tell themselves in front of a mirror that they are happy.

So, is there a way that you can embrace all this uncertainty that surrounds you and yet function at your best? There is no absolute answer to that but I believe First Principles Thinking will provide a significant push in this regard.

'First Principles Thinking' Simplified

First Principles Thinking, sometimes called 'reasoning from first principles,' is one of the most effective strategies you can employ to break down complex problems and generate original solutions. It may also be the best approach to learn how to think for yourself.

When you try to approach an issue through FPT, you can get to the crux and find your way around it with three smart, straightforward steps.

The first step in FPT is simple: question yourself. Ask yourself, "What if my assumptions about something are wrong?" Don't question yourself like an insecure person would, worrying about everything that could go wrong. Instead, question yourself with confidence and build on what you know and have done.

The second step is to look at the problem as is, stripped of all biases. Ask yourself, "What do I know about solving this problem that is absolutely true? Where can I generate data that will help me create solutions to this problem?" This step will help you set down a list of ideas or 'first principles.' This set of first principles then becomes the basis of your solution. Initially, it helps to generate at least two or three 'first principles'.

The third step is to look at all the first principles that you have generated and decide which is most likely to lead you to your best solution. The principles that you filter out needn't be completely ignored; sometimes, they provide inputs at a later stage that help you streamline your solution even further.

When you employ the solution, you generate the desired outcome which helps you eliminate the problem presented. If all of this looks quite complicated, worry not. The examples that we will look at as we go forward will help clarify the concept.

The first principles approach has been widely used by many great thinkers, right from Socrates and Aristotle to Buzzfeed creator Jonah Peretti and musician-cum-entrepreneur Derek Sivers, but no one has been a bigger example and a staunch follower of first principles thinking than Elon Musk.

Elon Musk and SpaceX

One person who never ceases to amaze me for the way he thinks and acts is Elon Musk. Musk has been quite a personality, and I love the way he operates, more so because he ardently follows the theory of FPT.

Back in 2002, when Musk decided to start a company by the name of 'Space Exploration Technologies' (SpaceX), his idea was merely to send people to Mars. When he approached people to understand the cost of a rocket, he was taken aback—he realized that the cost of buying a rocket was astronomical (pun intended): approximately 65 million USD. He decided he had to approach this problem with a fresh perspective. Here's a snippet from an interview he did in 2012 with Chris Anderson, the then editor-in-chief of *Wired*:

"I tend to approach things from a physics framework," Musk said in the interview. "Physics teaches you to reason from first principles rather than by analogy. So, I said, okay, let's look at the first principles. What is a rocket made of? Aerospace-grade aluminium alloys, plus some titanium, copper, and carbon fibre. Then I asked, what is the value of those materials on the commodity market? It turned out that the materials cost of a rocket was around two percent of the typical price."

This fact inspired him to start making his own rockets. He bought his own materials at the cheapest price possible and reinvented rocket design. It didn't take a long time for him to lower the cost of making rockets by nearly ten times and make some profit out of it too. It was clear that Musk had used the power of FPT to break down rocket-making to its bare basic principles, thus creating a more viable and cost-effective solution.

The Power of WHY

You may be wondering why FPT isn't spoken about more often if it is indeed such a powerful concept. The answer to this question is etched in our childhood. What if I told you that you applied FPT several years ago as a child? Yes! As children, we instinctively thought in terms of first principles. We always tried to understand what was happening around us. Sometimes when we didn't, we went ahead and relentlessly asked questions. The simplest and most powerful question we never failed to ask was 'WHY?'.

Here's a typical conversation that happens with my niece, Tvisha:

"Come on. Let's go back, Tvisha. We have been playing in the rain for more than an hour now."

"Why?" she promptly asks.

"Because we may catch a cold, and then it will make us sick."

"Why do we catch a cold?"

"Because our body isn't used to being wet for so long and our body doesn't like the change in temperature."

"Why can't we just take a hot bath later? Won't our body adjust the temperature back? Whenever my milk gets cold, my mom just heats it up!"

"Because our body doesn't react like milk, Tvisha!"

"Why not?"

She just wouldn't stop!

Children are always trying to understand the world around them and see why they do what they do. This is instinctive for them.

Most of us have enough patience to humour this barricade of questions perhaps a couple of times in a day. Beyond that though, we are probably going to respond with one of: "I don't know", "Because I said so!", or "It is just the way it is."

Slowly, growing up with these answers erodes the child's curiosity and his will to ask questions. So, does that mean that we need to think like a child when we work using FPT? Well, almost. Because you need to understand this:

The day you stop asking questions
is the day you lose your curiosity.

When an apple hit him on the head, if Newton had gone to his father and asked, "Why did an apple fall on me from the tree?", can you imagine what he would have been told? It might have been along the lines of "because it does!". Had he pestered his father more, and if his father was anybody like the typical Indian father in the 90s, all Isaac Newton would have got was another bump in the head, only this time it wouldn't have been because of an apple.

Weren't you too this way as a child? Wasn't it natural for you to question everything? Then somewhere along the way, didn't this curiosity just wither away? When was the last time you asked 'WHY' over and over again, even at the risk of being called stupid?

The biggest reason we lose the ability to question is the presence of authority figures—not just those in our childhood but even those who arrive much later. As a child, I am sure that we stopped questioning things because we were told "Because I said so!" most of the times. The same thing continued whenever our boss or an authority figure said, "Because that's how it works!"

When we refuse to accept something for what it already is, we often become the problem: we become the student who always irritates the teachers, we become the subordinate who just never does what he is told to do, we become the kid who never allows the parent to cook in peace.

If we never train ourselves to deconstruct a situation or phenomenon, isolate the assumptions behind it, and question or validate them through our own independent standards, then we are simply being led by what has already been established. The environment may change, but the pattern continues.

Many of us don't even realize it when we lose our curiosity and the natural ability to use FPT.

Without FPT, There Are Only Limiting Beliefs

"As to methods, there may be a million and then some, but principles are few. The man who grasps principles can successfully select his own methods. The man who tries methods, ignoring principles, is sure to have trouble."

Harrington Emerson

As kids, we had no problem giving an ambitious answer to the question, "What do you want to be when you grow up?" But the problem begins when we let others tell us what's possible, not only with respect to our dreams, but also how to go after them. When we let them do that, we start to follow their path. But more on that in Chapter 2.

When we let ourselves fall into the trap of believing what others think is right, we start using their analogies and their ideas to inhibit our vision and then end up getting stuck in their possibilities. Doesn't that seem a bit regressive?

There were enough people to tell Galileo that the Earth is the centre of the Universe. Did that make it right though?

The problem with our world is the imagined reality we live in. What looks right to most people is deemed correct, and what looks wrong to most people is deemed incorrect.

It is quite fascinating, and yet, at the same time, regressive that we decide what's right and wrong based on what others before us have claimed. If we are only going to improve upon something that already exists, we can never come up with an original solution. That is why these notions and assumptions that we believe to be true, become our biggest barriers. They become our limiting beliefs.

Let's now look at some common limiting beliefs we develop over time. Be honest with yourself when you read through these. See if you have entertained one or more of these beliefs at least once in your life or if you still hold them.

I don't have a good memory.

How good is one's memory? When evaluating our memory, many of us who have grown older start to believe with time that it isn't as good as it used to be. "I don't have a good memory" starts to become an excuse whenever we misplace something or forget a birthday. But actually, our memory is far better than we assume. Applying First Principles Thinking, we could begin by asking how much an average person can remember. This inquiry lets us realize that we can usually remember so much more than we think.

There is simply too much information out there.

I have observed that there are two kinds of professional investors who read *The Economic Times*. The first type claims there is too much information to consume. They spend their days reading every press release, article, and opinion piece. Even after doing that, they feel they may have misséd out on something. The second type of investor understands that it is practically not possible to read everything that is out there and that the curse of too much knowledge is real. These investors, by applying FPT, try to look at the information that the market may actually be sensitive to. They cut through all the irrelevant information and pay attention to what they really should. That is what makes them more successful.

We need to be the first mover.

Several phones existed before the iPhone, but the latter was so much more well-designed than all its predecessors. Amazon was not the first company to foray into e-commerce, but it became fast, agile, and ruthless and that has made it what it is today. A lot of evidence shows that the first movers in business fail more often than the latecomers, yet there is a frenzy to be the first to execute an idea.

At the end of the day, you need to break each situation down to its first principles to understand what works and what doesn't.

Applying FPT in Your Life

**"If I had an hour to solve a problem, I'd spend
fifty-five minutes thinking about the problem
and five minutes thinking about solutions."**

Albert Einstein

Let us now understand a practical methodology to apply FPT in our lives. Here's a simple three-step method to quickly apply FPT.

STEP 1: Define your problem along with its underlying assumptions.

Defining the problem in the form of a clear problem statement is the simplest step in the FPT process. I have listed below three problem statements that will be later solved using FPT.

Problem Statement 1: "The attrition rate in a small organization is high."

Problem Statement 2: "I lack the creativity to do something different."

Problem Statement 3: "Dieting is difficult."

Go ahead and write down the problem statements of the main issues that you seek to solve. Then, write down the current assumptions you have about the problem. Try to probe deep and list down at least three assumptions. For example, consider problem statement 3. People generally have three assumptions when they want to go on a diet:

There must be some level of motivation to go on a diet.

Going on a diet is taxing.

One must starve themselves on a diet.

It is important that you do justice to the process of introspection because from the assumptions arises an understanding of the core principles, and from the principles will arise the solution.

When you work out a solution, you will keep referring to the assumptions that you had. It is not that all the assumptions you have about a problem are wrong. It is just that you are blinded by them and find it difficult to look past them. And when you look at these assumptions in a different light, you get to the root of the solution—the first principles.

Assumptions don't necessarily have to be wrong statements or not be a part of your solution to a problem. Assumptions are usually statements that people have made about a problem that you believe to be true. But when you actually test these assumptions and find them to be an appropriate approach to a solution, they may even become your first principles. Simply speaking, assumptions can also be a part of your solution but only when you are able to verify them with your own logic and application.

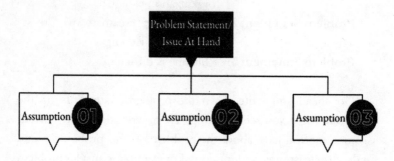

STEP 2: Use fundamental principles to break down the problem.

"It is important to view knowledge as a sort of semantic tree. Make sure you understand the fundamental principles, that is, the trunk and big branches, before you get into the leaves/details or there is nothing for them to hang on to."

Elon Musk

The fundamental principles behind a process are its most basic truths or elements.

Just as the leaves of a tree are anchored by its trunk and branches, the solutions to a problem start to appear when you work from fundamental principles.

The best way to uncover these truths is to ask powerful questions. Here's a quick note from Elon Musk during an interview with Kevin Rose on how this works.

"Somebody could say, 'Battery packs are really expensive and that's just the way they will always be. Historically, it has cost $600 per kilowatt hour. It's not going to be much better than that in the future.'

"With first principles, you say, 'What are the material constituents of the batteries? What is the stock market value of the material constituents?' It's got cobalt, nickel, aluminium, carbon, some polymers for separation, and a seal can. Break that down on a material basis and say, 'If we bought that on the London Metal Exchange, what would each of those things cost?'

"It's like $80 per kilowatt hour. So clearly you just need to think of clever ways to take those materials and combine them into the shape of a battery cell, and you can have batteries that are much, much cheaper than anyone realizes."

What Musk has said completely captures the essence of FPT.

Instead of buying the common wisdom that battery packs will be expensive, Musk asked some essential questions that uncovered the basic elements behind them, which are carbon, nickel, and aluminium. Then, he created ingenious, innovative solutions from scratch.

STEP 3: Build new solutions created from scratch.

"The person who says he knows what he thinks but Wcannot express it usually does not know what he thinks."

Mortimer Adler

Once you've identified the assumptions and broken down the problem into the most basic principles, you can generate a solution that is insightful. These solutions need not be innovative or complicated. In fact, they are often the opposite—they are simple and clear. That is the power of First Principles Thinking.

Through these solutions, you get a desired outcome which either solves the problem or shows you the right direction to solve it.

Let us understand this with a small flow chart, and then we will apply FPT to the problems mentioned earlier.

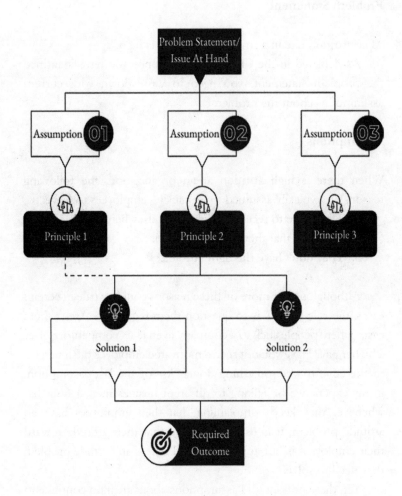

Let us understand the methodology in a step-by-step manner with an example.

Problem Statement

"The attrition rate in a small organization is high."

As depicted in the FPT flow chart, once you have identified the problem statement, you need to write down your current assumptions about the problem.

Assumptions

When there is high attrition at an organization, the following reasons are typically assumed to be causing employees to leave:

1. They leave to receive a higher pay elsewhere.
2. They feel that they are overworked.
3. They don't have the right attitude.

Although one or more of these reasons could be true in certain cases, the rule in FPT is to question them regardless. Aren't there cases where people stick to a company even if its competitors offer a higher pay? Have you not seen a motivated employee push herself to the edge to get something done? As for the last assumption, in my experience of talking to different businessmen, I find that whenever they keep complaining that their employees have an attitude problem, it is usually the case that their attitude toward their employees is not appropriate and that is an attitude problem they need to solve.

Yet, these notions and assumptions about attrition continue to be unquestioned by many.

After you write down the assumptions, you need to break down the problem into fundamental principles and write these down.

Fundamental Principles

For the problem of attrition, let us look into what the underlying principles could be. The attrition rate could be high in an organization due to many reasons. But for the sake of argument here, let us look at some thoughts I believe could contribute to a reduction of attrition rate in medium and small businesses. These thoughts will form the basis of our first principles.

> **Principle 1:** The organization doesn't hire the right people for the right position.
>
> **Principle 2:** The organization doesn't give employees enough challenges to learn new things.
>
> **Principle 3:** There isn't a satisfactory growth plan for employees in the organization.

The solution can be generated using one or more principles from the above list, but the first task is to find one core principle in the list that can generate the best insight toward finding a solution for the given problem.

The other principles may be supportive and a good way to start is to eliminate the principles that will not help us find the solution. Which principle becomes the core principle is highly case specific. For example, not all attrition-related problems in all organizations will have the same core principle leading to a solution. In the above example, let us consider the principles one by one.

When considering the first principle, an employer may feel that he has an extensive hiring process and that he usually gets the right people for the right position, and hence decide to eliminate that principle from the consideration set.

With regard to principles 2 and 3, an employer may realize that there is monotony in how people work at his organization and that there are no adequate growth plans for employees.

Hence, in this case, the employer may decide to look at how he can improve the work environment and provide more challenges to his employees.

Solution

1. Sit with employees and collaboratively chart out a growth plan for them.
2. Look to increase the responsibilities that each employee has so that they are engaged efficiently.

The Outcome

By applying FPT to the problem, an employer can break it down into its fundamental principles and come up with a solution that can provide a unique outcome; the employer can now take these effective steps to reduce attrition at his organization.

When an employer is able to have this conversation with the employees, it gives the employees an impetus to work harder towards the growth of the organization too.

There is a possibility that the employer can come up with this solution even without applying FPT. Yet, it is possible that he may have his thoughts confounded by several other assumptions—his own and what he had heard from other people in his trade.

This clarity of thought is what you get when you apply FPT to even the simplest of problems with an evident solution. Musk didn't do anything extraordinary by breaking down the elements of a battery pack, looking at its material costs, and then understanding that it doesn't have to be so expensive. But the methods he used to reach this conclusion are what made the solution so powerful!

Let us now also look at how all this data would look in the FPT flow chart. Further, we will employ the same method in the other two examples to understand the concept better.

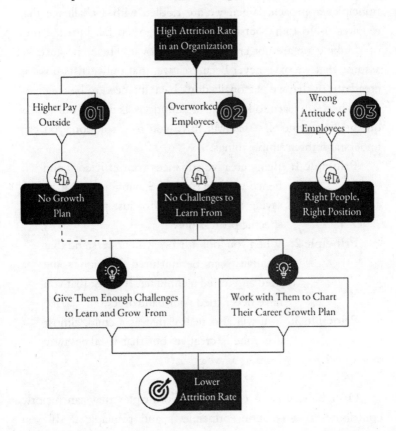

Solving Problem 2

Let us now derive a solution for another problem through the first principles approach. When we are riddled with a challenge that requires us to think outside the box, we often fall into the trap of thinking we are not creative enough for it. This is because we assume that we have never been creative, that only artists possess creativity, or that we personally don't have the need to be creative.

When you learn to keep the assumptions aside and only focus on the first principles that will drive you to a solution, you can understand three simple things:

Principle 1: Being creative enhances your efficiency and hence you can't escape having a go at it by saying that it is meant for just people of a specific profession.

Principle 2: When you look further, you understand that creativity can be nurtured through some tried and tested techniques. It is just that you have never tried your hand at it.

Principle 3: You will also realize that as a child, almost everyone is creative, but that is taken away from us as we grow.

Over here, we can consider two principles that can majorly contribute to a solution: principle 1 and principle 2. If you consistently work on some techniques of creativity and try to include them even in small aspects of everyday life, you will be better able to bring out your creativity.

The desired outcome through this is that you will be able to include creativity as a part of your daily life, and this will enhance your productivity and sharpen your mind.

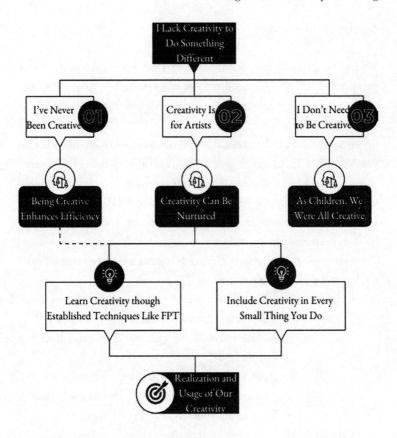

Solving Problem 3

These days, dieting has become more a necessity than just a fancy thing to try. With changing nutritional availability, especially, and a lifestyle that requires less physical activity, dieting seems to have become a priority for many.

But one aspect that certainly seems to have not changed is that people still wait to get motivated to go on a diet as if it were a prerequisite of some sort. And this is our first assumption—that motivation is an important factor of going on a diet—followed by other notions such as going on a diet is taxing and that one needs to starve themselves on a diet.

When we take a step back and ask what are the first principles to do on a diet, we discover these:

Principle 1: More than being the driver, motivation becomes a mental block when it comes to dieting because we wait for it to even start our diet.

Principle 2: A diet can always be worked out to suit a person's existing lifestyle, conditions, and local or seasonal availability of food.

Principle 3: There are now more than enough well-established diet practices that one can choose among.

And when we try to understand and work on a solution from our principles, we understand that a diet doesn't necessarily have to be a completely charted out plan, and that it can be a part of our daily eating routine. Apart from that, there is always the option of taking up a diet plan to see if it works for us and then deciding whether to continue it or not.

The outcome, naturally, is that you develop a stress-free diet plan that helps nurture your body while also keeping you in shape.

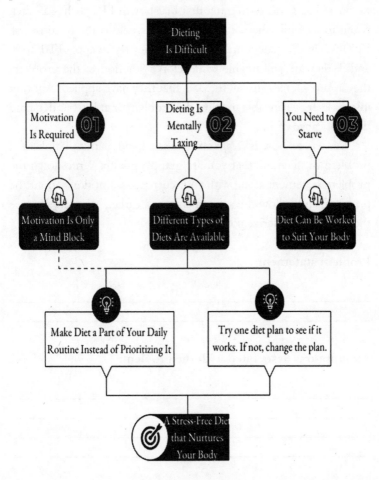

I hope the examples provide you a head start at understanding how FPT works and how you can apply it in your life. At my workplace and home, I have applied FPT successfully and gotten solutions to problems that had bothered me for years.

I have personally trained my employees in the concepts of first principles thinking. When they first heard about it, they were as fascinated as I was during my first brush with FPT. It has, in fact, come to a point where all my employees talk to me in terms of FPT. When they encounter a problem, they try to apply FPT to it, and if they are still unable to develop a solution to the problem, they approach me with all the data that they have applied. Another insight later, we are able to solve the problem or at least understand the root cause of it.

Let us see now if you can try your hand at this. Think of a problem or dilemma that you are grappling with. Write down the problem statement along with your current assumptions about the problem, and follow the steps mentioned earlier. You can also use the flowchart to derive your solutions.

Problem statement:

_____

_____

Assumptions associated with the problem:

_____

_____

_____

_____

Underlying fundamental principles:

_____

_____

_____

Solutions derived from the principles:

_____

_____

Unique/required outcome:

_____

Conclusion

**What we believe outside of our own
understanding will only imprison us.**

At the end of the day, FPT really just does one thing: it makes your thinking a more expansive process. People are generally constrained because of assumptions that they just can't seem to let go of.

When you break down a problem into first principles, you start letting go of misguided or faulty assumptions. That's when you realize that the way you were working on something for so long was never right.

Ideally, you should use FPT when:

1. You are looking at a complex problem.
2. You are dealing with something you have never done before.
3. You want a fresh perspective on a problem you haven't been able to solve.

In all these situations, it helps if you are able to keep your assumptions aside and stop looking at the problem from someone else's perspective.

Understanding something with an open mind is always better than looking at it through an analogy. For example, there will always be a set of people who will tell you their version of why something can't be done based on their experiences. But let me drop a truth bomb here. I have observed that whenever people say, "that's how it works," most of the time, it is not based on their experiences but based on what they heard from someone else. Whatever had limited them for so long now limits you.

This thought is perfectly portrayed through the achievement of the four-minute mile by Roger Bannister on May 6, 1954. Right until that day, people thought it was physically impossible for a human being to run a mile under four minutes. Thus, it was more a psychological barrier than a physical one. Bannister achieved this feat by not following any ideas that already existed and didn't believe in the existing coaching methods of running that people followed back then. The press and the people constantly used to criticize his 'lone wolf' approach.

What's more intriguing is that experts believed they knew the precise conditions under which one would be able to run a mile within four minutes. It would have to be on a day with perfect weather—the temperature hovering around 20 degrees Celsius, with minimum wind. They believed the feat would have to be completed on a hard, dry clay running track with a boisterous crowd cheering the runner to perform his best. But against all logic, Bannister achieved this feat on a cold day surrounded by a crowd of just a few thousand people on a wet track!

If you look at how he achieved this feat, wouldn't you say that the way Bannister followed his own methods of working out and didn't believe in doing it on a 'perfect' day made this feat even more remarkable? Surely, he might not have known what FPT was then but he still followed the same principles in doing what he did.

When we remove that hazy screen and look at things the way they really are by using FPT, most things suddenly seem possible.

I decided to write this book because I was tired of living in a world of cliched analogy and assumptions. I wanted to take a step back and look at life with a fresh perspective. Through a thorough understanding of FPT, along with some other experiences, I gained a lot of clarity on my old patterns.

For example, my father was the reason I restricted myself from getting into business partnerships—simply because partnerships didn't work for him. My mother's insecurities were the reason I never instinctively trusted people. I grew up hearing so many stories about people having betrayed her, and hence, being on guard became my instinctive way of approaching people. Some of my teachers were the reason I was always afraid to take risks in life—simply because they never let me take any. The list goes on and on.

The moment I took a step out of this vicious circle of analogies and assumptions, I was able to create a new world for myself. And I realized one very important thing:

Complexity lies in the way we see problems, and not in the solutions.

The moment I looked at problems as mere problems and not as unsolvable entities, things became clearer. Life became easy, not because I stopped having problems but because I became more focused on solutions.

This book is an effort to bring that clarity to you; to give you a glimpse of what happens when you stop being constrained by all that you have been doing for so long and start looking at what more could be possible for you.

I hope that you receive the same joy and clarity on this journey that I have reaped for the last three years—by learning, unlearning, breaking down, and rebuilding everything. Life is nothing but a canvas of which we are a small but important part. Let's look at what we can do for ourselves rather than have others tell us what we should do. In short, let us love living.

Here's a small poem I wrote—my ode to your promising journey that begins right now.

Problems aren't small, and sadness isn't far,
But let life not leave a scar,
Say goodbye to that misery from afar.

Life will try to get to you someday,
Look at it in the eyes and say NOT TODAY,
And make today more memorable than YESTERDAY.

It's easy to crib, cry, and whine,
But remember NOW is your time to shine,
And leave your footprints on the sands of time.

Don't let anger and pain make you sink,
Because life is much shorter than you think,
It might all go away in just a blink.

Let's stop cringing,
And instead of just wishing,
Let's LOVE LIVING.

Chapter Summary

- The clarity we have as children turns into confusion as we grow old.
- The right way to deal with uncertainties is by acknowledging them instead of denying that they exist.
- First Principles Thinking is a three-step process: remove assumptions by questioning them, find the first principles of a problem, use the insight to generate a solution.
- Without FPT, sometimes we get lost in our limiting beliefs as we consider the current situation as a norm.
- Removing assumptions requires you to question yourself to understand the truth behind something. Asking yourself WHY repeatedly usually helps.
- Usually, one of the first principles generated becomes the insight.
- The solution will give rise to the required outcome that you want.
- At the end of the day, FPT really just does one thing: it makes your thinking a more expansive process.
- The moment you look at problems as mere problems and not as unsolvable entities, things became clearer.

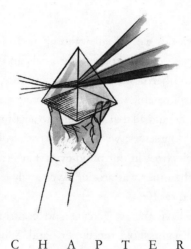

C H A P T E R

2

A Purpose That Fires You Up

"Understanding purpose is one thing, but recognizing the
importance of having a purpose is another."

Ben Gothard

Do You Create Your Purpose or Does Your Purpose Create You?

In an ideal world, we will all wake up with a single-minded, exhilarating sense of purpose. Our goals and choices will be consistent and harmonious with one another, devoid of any loose ends. We will be able to derive a meaning in all that we have accomplished so far and all that we intend to accomplish. However, if we are true to ourselves, we know this is hardly the case. On many days, there's chaos in our mind even if it's calm outside. On some days, it is the other way around. We slowly learn to live with it. But do we ever, really?

We often believe that we create and control our thoughts. However, our thoughts hold the upper hand. When we wish for clarity, we get confused. When we wish for structure, we get chaos. When we wish for positivity, we drown in self-doubt. And amidst all the botch-ups in our planning, execution, and effort, life happens. As if our own mind doesn't cause enough havoc, there are also others telling us that what we do is not good enough and we should lead our lives differently.

People keep talking to us about goals, targets, and achievements in a manner that suggests that if we don't have these, we are crazy. Secure the first rank in your grade, score above 90% in all your subjects, maintain your BMI below 25, ensure satisfactory performance at all your KPIs, achieve 30% annual growth for your business, ensure the bottom line is higher than last year's, and so on. The list never ends, does it?

I agree that challenges can be beneficial. When one isn't challenged enough, it is easy to start losing the zest to perform. But how can we steer the course of life with confidence amidst these challenges? The resounding answer is: by developing an invincible sense of purpose.

What you constantly refer to, believe in, or create your standards in accordance with is your purpose. Purpose, simply put, is the reason why something is created or accomplished.

A strong sense of purpose is why Martin Luther King Jr. decided to change the way a nation treated a particular race. Purpose is why Steve Jobs decided to challenge the status quo of technology as we know it. Purpose is why Simon Sinek chose to inspire people to create 'derived change.' Amongst everything else that purpose is, there is one aspect that's clear:

The pursuit of purpose is never-ending.

People tend to think that purpose is a life-long approach to achieving one thing. I think otherwise. Purpose, I believe, is not a singular goal or destination that one wishes to reach. Purpose is about living every day in the best possible manner, believing in yourself, and making things happen with what you have. Purpose is not a goal; it is a sense of direction. Purpose is not a destination; it is a journey.

When Elon Musk created PayPal, a program that completely changed how payments were made, did he stop at it? When he decided to challenge the conventional means of driving by making Tesla one of the best car companies in the world, did he stop there? He decided to get people to space so that humans could inhabit Mars. Now that he has started his journey toward achieving that, does he get complacent? Musk is constantly evolving his methods, and along with them, the way we live. Elon Musk's purpose is to create such a massive difference in the way the world works that we wait with bated breath to see what he will do next. His purpose is to not stop at one thing. And that is why having a sense of purpose changes your perspective of life altogether. But what does one's purpose comprise, really?

Components of Purpose

Purpose comprises two components: the 'What' and the 'Why.' 'What' is your routine: actions that you perform day in and day out. 'Why' is your general sense of direction in life. It is the more critical part of your purpose because it provides a sense of fulfilment and meaning to life.

Steve Jobs was a marketing genius, but he was also someone uncompromising of mediocrity. His What was to create wonderful products with advanced technology. His What was also to get the best out of the people who worked for him. Some might say that he was a difficult leader to work with. Well, that's because of his Why. To Jobs, it was important to challenge the status quo at every step along the way, be it at making products or getting things done from people. He wasn't going to compromise on either, and he made sure that the people around him understood this. Having said that, we need to understand the structure and importance of the 'What' and the 'Why' to get a deeper understanding of purpose.

A Formula for Purpose

$$\text{Purpose} = (\text{What})^{(\text{Why})}$$

Purpose is your What to the power of your Why. In other words, the strength of your purpose significantly increases when your Why becomes stronger. This is why defining your Why is important. The same thoughts were reiterated by the popular author and speaker Simon Sinek, when he created the *Golden Circle* model, in which he says:

"Always start with Why!"

It has been a lifelong journey for Simon Sinek to help people find their Why. He believes that if you start acting in alignment with your Why, you will find fulfilment in your actions. Finding your Why is not easy. It takes an organized, deeply introspective approach. This chapter will guide you to connect the dots that will eventually lead you to your Why. We will talk more about this later. First, let us look at some common hindrances that prevent most of us from seeing our purpose clearly.

The Primary Obstacle to Finding Our Purpose

Why is it generally difficult for so many people to find a purpose that brings clarity and joy? I believe it's because we are drowned in the sea of societal opinions—opinions that lead our thoughts astray and alienate us from our sense of identity.

I also believe that life gives most of us enough opportunities to do more, learn more, and fulfil our purpose. And yet, few people proceed to pursue this path.

Most of us get lost along the way to finding our purpose because our purpose somehow becomes a by-product of circumstances and not something pursued with intent. We get trapped in the societal message that our purpose is to work hard, earn money, keep everyone around us happy, earn more money, gain respect, and then, earn some more money.

Targets have been provided to us right from childhood, and somehow, we start to believe that the purpose of our life is to achieve these. For a while now, I have avoided the numbers game.

This doesn't mean I don't look at numbers; it just means I don't give them the importance that many people do. I look at numbers to gain an understanding, but I never look at them as targets. We need to understand where we are headed and if we are doing better than before, but there is no point getting obsessed over these details. Not every day will be the same, not every month will be productive, and not every year will provide the same quantity or quality of results.

When you observe this kind of behaviour through First Principles Thinking, doesn't earning money sound like one of those assumptions that you have without deliberation?

Getting out of this trap doesn't look that easy. Still, we could all at least start to understand the challenges and priorities that currently define our days. We could begin by understanding our What, and our What is determined by our day-to-day priorities.

Understanding You're What from Your Priorities

You don't need to go about setting priorities. The good news is that you already have priorities, regardless of whether they are aligned to the right Why. Simply put, your current priorities are how you spend your time at present. How do you usually spend your days? What do you do to keep yourself engaged? What do you do to gain financial security? What daily action of yours makes you and your close ones happy? What do you do to become more (or less) social? These are pretty simple questions to answer, and they will give you an idea of who you are in the context of a routine. After all, most of us unwittingly follow a routine every day.

For example, I generally wake up by 6.15 a.m. At that quiet time of the day, I focus on getting some writing done. Our family then gathers for a small prayer, after which, we try to make it a point to have breakfast together and talk about each other's plans for the day as it makes us feel more connected. Once breakfast is done, I head to my office. At the office, there's a lot of delegation and some interaction with customers to check if their requirements are being met. In the afternoon, I write again or introspect on certain issues. Later in the evening, I go back home to my family and spend the rest of the evening with them—a time that includes a bit of television, a bit of catching up, and a lot of quality time, overall. Then I am off to bed, and I wake up the next morning and get back to my routine.

I am sure many of you have a similar pattern that works with a slightly different list of activities.

Now that you understand what your current tasks and priorities look like, let me ask you a question: Are these the priorities you ideally want to accommodate for the rest of your life?

We could be doing certain activities repeatedly because we have been trained (yes, you read it right) to do so. Sometimes we find happiness in our routine and sometimes we don't. But to increase the probability that we do, we need to introspect a little. It is important to understand what we look forward to in our lives. That answer can be arrived at by asking this simple question:

Where do you see yourself headed in the long term with all your current efforts?

I once read a study that said that most people have 75% of their day lodged into a routine, and it is what they do with the remaining 25% of their time that determines their direction in life. Simply put, your priorities point to what challenges you wish to solve in the near future.

To help elaborate this further, I will now recount a story.

"Can you show him around your factory and spend some time with him, Sagar?" asked Mohan Uncle.

Mohan Uncle is one of our vendors. My dad used to outsource his work to Mohan Uncle's dad, and now I do the same with Mohan Uncle. That's how long back we go. So, naturally, when Mohan Uncle asked me to show his friend's son, Shashank, around my plant, I was more than happy to do it.

At first glance, Shashank looked like an exuberant young man. He was stepping into his final year of college and was trying to evaluate his options for further studies.

Shashank's father was a multimillionaire who oversaw a business that operated at a global scale. I had heard stories about his father from Mohan Uncle. Shashank's father had humble beginnings and had started his business from scratch when he was quite young. He knew that a wide breadth of knowledge was important for Shashank's growth. So, when Shashank planned a trip to Chennai, his father wanted him to go and explore the working of different industries so that Shashank could study how other organizations operated.

Shashank spent his morning around Mohan Uncle's factory, and our meeting was planned for the afternoon. After introducing us informally, Mohan Uncle bid goodbye to us. "Take good care of him, Sagar," he said as he left.

Early on during our interaction, Shashank seemed shy. He was not the easiest person to strike a conversation with and came across as introverted. Alas, he didn't realize he was with someone who was quite adept at dealing with introverts, thanks to Mrs. Sagar!

After some small talk about college life and such, I showed him around my factory. He was intrigued by our manufacturing process and asked a lot of questions (Pro tip: If you ever meet a shy or introverted person and want to get them to talk, try making them curious.). Shashank continued with his questions, and I answered them as patiently as I could. Watching Shashank also made me nostalgic: when I was in college, I did the same when I visited other people's factories.

During lunch, we started to discuss topics apart from work. I told him about my family: my love story is fodder for entertainment in most casual conversations. I tried to keep it short, but his curiosity led him to ask more and more questions. Eventually, he began to get comfortable and spoke about his father, their business, and his plans.

"Dad feels that the company currently needs a good marketing professional at the helm," Shashank said. "So, I am thinking of pursuing my master's degree in marketing and dedicating my time to the company."

"Have you been visiting your company regularly?" I asked.

"Yes, I spent quite a few days there last summer. This year, I plan to spend the entire summer there to wrap my head around how things work."

"Interesting," I thought aloud. "And what have you observed from your visits?"

"I have been trying to understand the operations and observe how things get done. It has been interesting, but I haven't been able to contribute much."

"Only if you observe can you contribute, Shashank. Anyway, did you observe and understand how marketing works in your industry and how you will fit in that role?"

"No, not really. The other day, Dad and I were talking, trying to understand where I would be a good fit. He felt that I could do well in marketing."

"Okay. And what do you think?" I probed.

"Well. Right now, I am not so sure. Maybe I will do well in marketing. But I am fascinated by numbers, and I think I would want to do something in finance."

"That's good! Then why do you want to take up a master's degree in marketing?"

"I don't know, Sagar. I feel Dad knows what's best for me.

And shouldn't I be looking at what's good for the company? If the company needs support in marketing, I am doing the right thing by going in that direction, right?"

"How so?" I probed further.

"Because, um . . . my father thinks so?"

He knew something wasn't right here. I smiled wryly at him. I knew it wasn't my place to tell him if he was right or wrong in following his father's directions rather than his own instinct. But I hoped that our conversation stirred his thoughts a little so that he could think more clearly. He was clearly falling into the trap of "Because they said so!" and it was important for someone to let him know that he didn't have to do something because someone said so. Maybe he wanted to hear that too. Maybe this was the validation that he was seeking.

In this incident, Shashank's 'What' was staring him in the face. He wanted to contribute to his company's growth by working in finance. However, he was already shrouded by his father's ideas about him doing better at marketing. If he took up marketing, he would still be contributing to the company. But will it be of the same magnitude as would be the case if he worked in finance, a field that fascinated him? Probably not.

The reason he would be better off choosing finance over marketing is simple: the challenge it offers. The challenges that he wishes to solve are in finance. He is naturally inclined towards these, so he will likely do a better job.

If Shashank chooses to work in finance, who will take care of marketing, one might wonder. Ideally, it should be someone whose 'What' lies in marketing.

When Steve Jobs and Steve Wozniak started a company, Jobs let Wozniak handle the tech department, while he took up marketing. Imagine if the roles had been reversed. Imagine if Jobs had been pushed to focus completely on technology. Perhaps Apple Inc., as we know it today, wouldn't have existed.

A key pointer to healthy priorities is those challenges that make you sit up eagerly and lead you to believe that you can contribute meaningfully. There are different ways in which you can contribute to your existing job and portfolio. There are different areas at which you can excel, and few areas that will naturally fascinate you. It is up to you to find them and work with them. It all depends on the challenges you desire to take up and the problems you wish to solve. Remember, your challenges determine your priorities, and your priorities determine your What.

Before we proceed, I want you to write down three priorities that you desire to hold at this point in life. While you do this exercise, I suggest that you take some time off, sit in a silent corner, and truly look within. Can you think beyond what's considered right or successful by the world at large? Can you reflect deeply on what makes you feel joyous and competent? Think about the challenges that you wish to solve. Think about the pain you don't mind undergoing to overcome these challenges.

Also, among these three priorities, I suggest that you write at least one that is not related to your work or family so that there is at least one priority that focuses just on yourself. List the priorities alongside the broad category they fall under. The following were my priorities at the time of writing this book:

1. **Business Development:** Add at least two major customers to our portfolio in the next six months.
2. **Family:** Spend enough time with my wife, Devangee, and provide adequate care and support in the upbringing of our son, Aarav.
3. **Myself:** Finish writing this book and publish it by the end of 2022.

You can write more priorities if you want to, but I suggest you write at least three.

Now, list down your priorities in a similar manner below:

Your Priorities:

When you set your priorities based on your strengths, free from the trap of assumptions and influence, you will experience a certain amount of ease and joy. More often than not, these priorities will be different from what others expect of you. The ease and joy arise from working with your intuition, the gut instinct generated from your limbic brain. The limbic brain is that part of your brain that helps you decide based on not just what seems practical but also what truly makes you happy.

But for most of us, because of how we have been conditioned since childhood, it becomes difficult to look past practicality. We fall into a trap of manufactured Whats that usually derail us.

We tend to keep at this game until we realize that we have been playing it wrong all along. It is this moment of awareness that gives our life meaning. As I had mentioned earlier, self-awareness is a gift. And until we fully manifest this gift, we look to short-term goals to keep ourselves happy. But we can certainly do better than that.

Your Why Is Not What
You Imagined It to Be!

Imagine that you are on an adventure trip with a group of friends out in the woods. The sun has set, and all your phones have died. Your group is looking to reach a particular campsite, and you are all clearly lost. You have two tools to help you:

1. A map that provides a detailed picture of the area but doesn't contain the exact location of the campsite
2. A compass and a set of instructions that will guide you to your campsite

Let us understand the difference between the two tools.

A map provides a general idea about the landscape and location, while a compass can guide you in the right direction. A map contains a set of consistent symbols and representations that are quite easy to understand or interpret. But to use a compass, it is important to have a set of instructions to guide you to the destination. A map provides a sense of safety, whereas a compass could sometimes lead you into difficult terrain.

Now, one of your friends suggests that your group should split into two. Everyone agrees, and you split yourselves into Group A and Group B. Each group can pick one of the two tools to find the campsite.

Group A picks the map and wanders away. They believe that a sound knowledge of their surroundings will make it easier to navigate their way in the forest, and even if they don't know the exact location of the campsite, they will get lucky and eventually find it.

Group B, on the other hand, chooses to work with the compass and the set of instructions. They believe that the challenges that they may encounter due to the uncertain knowledge of their surroundings can be tackled, but it is important to know that they are headed in the right direction.

Which group will you opt to be a part of? And which group do you think will reach the campsite first?

In my opinion, it is important that you choose to work with a compass and a set of instructions. Because without a compass, a map loses its meaning, but without a map, a compass can still guide you in the right direction if you have an accurate set of instructions pointing you toward the destination.

What does any of this have to do with purpose? It is quite simple. In life, maps are like the advice that you receive over the years. The map is a landscape of all the Whats of others: you look in front of you and see some recommended career paths and objectives. You look to your right and find a set of personal goals cherished by society, stamped with a precise timeline. This landscape stretches endlessly. But unless the map is aligned with your own experience, these Whats become less effective. In short, if you start living your life based on someone else's experience, you will be living someone else's life. You need to remember that what works for others may or may not work for you.

When you let a compass and a set of instructions guide you instead, things start to look different. The compass in the example corresponds to your internal compass—a set of thoughts and feelings that strongly grip you. To follow your internal compass is to look at the world through your limbic brain and follow your instincts. Your instincts will guide you in the right direction, and that makes all the difference to living well.

**Your internal compass is the difference between
you choosing one path over another, sometimes
even without a sound reason.**

The tricky part about using your internal compass is that it may sometimes lead you into difficult situations. But you will learn from these experiences. Also, these experiences will become the guide to your Why and, eventually, your purpose. These experiences will be uniquely yours, and no one can take them away from you.

A powerful example of this is the story of Oprah Winfrey. Oprah has inspired many broken and dejected people to regain control over their lives. She has been able to accomplish this due to the lessons she learned from her own difficult past. She derived power from her pain and learned to cultivate empathy toward the common man. This made her who she is today. Her instinct told her to always be in touch with her humane side. When you couple that with the kind of experiences that she has had, you see why it led to strength, grit, and empathy. There are different ways that people can interpret her approach and style, but no one can deny that she has met with a lot of hardships, and it takes a lot to be who she is despite all that she has faced. Her What was always to connect with people and help them. Her Why became a journey to become someone empathetic and inspiring.

To reiterate what we have discussed, the map is a set of Whats that others follow. Alas, it obscures the understanding of our purpose. Others tell us what works and what doesn't, they tell us what is right and what isn't, but they can't help us to understand our purpose.

This is how I led a major part of my life. I was living out the map that was handed over to me by my father. It felt nice to be surrounded by my dad's wisdom right until I started my own business. Back in 2015, I started a factory that manufactured automobile components. My dad was well experienced in running a factory, and he was a hands-on manager. He was always on the shop floor getting his hands dirty and solving problems. That was his internal compass. Having come from a humble background, this strategy had helped him grow. He handed down his compass to me, thinking it would guide me, too. He wasn't wrong in thinking so. Unfortunately, his compass acted as a map for me. I wasn't comfortable being hands-on with everything, and even though the strategy of being hands-on continued to work and our business grew, I felt lost. I realized that I needed to develop my own sense of direction using my internal compass. Only, I didn't know what my compass was trying to show me.

Let us see how this scenario will play out in the corporate world, shall we?

According to a study by the Boston Consulting Group, the foremost complaint of employees at MNCs is that their bosses don't communicate the team's mission clearly. As a result, the employees don't know what their objectives are. This results in the executives getting lost in the details of extensive planning and strategies. They keep coming up with new ideas just to hide the lack of a clear objective. They get lost in the map without a clear destination. They act like Group A of our example. They know how to apply strategies, but they aren't sure if the strategies will help them achieve their objective. Companies like Nokia and Kodak, which failed to see what hit them when the world changed, are classic examples of the Group A strategy. Do you think they lacked good employees or products or effective marketing strategies? No. They faltered because their top management refused to steer the company using a compass. They were lost in the map and lost sight of their destination.

The employees at more successful companies act like Group B. They are clear about their objectives. Sometimes, they may not have strategies that are ready for implementation, but they have the right guidance to create new ones along the way. While trying to achieve their objectives, they may face some challenges and hurdles. But their ideas and thoughts are aligned in a manner such that by tweaking their strategy, they eventually achieve their objectives. Apple Inc. is an excellent example of a company that constantly improvises how they look at technology, and, in turn, how their customers perceive them. They navigate based on what's the right thing to do instead of falling into the trap of the map.

This is why it is important, for both organizations and individuals, to have an internal compass—a sound instinct of what's best for them. A strong internal compass leads us to our Why.

A Closer Look at Your Why

Earlier in the chapter, I had mentioned that your Why stems from the limbic part of your brain, whose function is to focus on what brings happiness rather than operate based on logic alone. Sometimes, this Why makes all the difference in the world. You are always going to do things that are a part of your priorities, but what if—for the sake of argument—you start working on priorities that give you happiness? Doesn't that change the whole question of being fulfilled in your life? Of course, it does. Thus the WHY part of the purpose becomes so important. Your Why simultaneously gives you a profound sense of both clarity and purpose. Your Why makes your preferences so clear that you don't have to think twice before choosing something. At the risk of sounding dramatic, let me say this: I believe that your Why is so powerful that it will not let you rest during the day; but the moment you lie on the bed at night, the sense of satisfaction of working from a Why perspective will bring good sleep even before you know it. Let me explain with an example.

Climbing Mount Everest is extremely challenging, and lots of people have lost their lives in the process. Yet, during the climbing season, people line up to climb Everest. This is probably because these people have a clear sense of their Why. Their Why is to surmount the insurmountable. With this strong sense of Why, they are able to overcome the fear of death itself. And once they achieve this feat, they will move on to the next challenge because their Why is clear. This is what I meant when I said early in this chapter that the pursuit of Why is never-ending.

The catch, though, is that finding your Why isn't all that easy. Because your Why is something so deep and powerful, it can't be achieved or understood over a day or through a single task.

But the good news is that we are going to try hard to find it. In the pursuit of your Why, I assure you that many doors will open for you. The pursuit of your Why will give you a sense of conviction that never existed before.

The Internal Compass Guides You to Your Why

Your internal compass refers to those instincts and inclinations that push you in the direction of your Why. Simply speaking, your internal compass helps you connect your What to your Why.

What → Internal Compass → Why

To find your internal compass, answer these three simple questions.

1. What challenges do you pursue that others are afraid to take up?

In the pursuit of your Why, you need to be mindful of those challenges that attract you, although most others don't find them worth taking on. For example, some people adore animals more than they do fellow humans. Some will do anything to protect the environment. Some others will stand up for what they believe in, no matter what the cost. They are often ridiculed as outcasts. But I call them people who truly believe in what they do—people who have found their internal compass.

2. What comes naturally to you?

Some people can sing. Some can dance. There are some who can move a crowd to tears with their words. Some are able to easily solve complex mathematical and scientific problems. We have all been given different gifts, and it is up to us to identify and nurture them. As life proceeds, these gifts, big or small, become a part of our internal compass.

3. What makes you happy even though you can't explain why?

To explain this question, I would like to talk about a gentleman named Pradeep John alias the Tamil Nadu Weatherman. A self-declared pluviophile, Pradeep was obsessed with the science of rainfall. He started a Facebook page to keep people updated on the rainfall patterns in the city of Chennai. Not a lot of people would have developed this kind of passion. His interest toward meteorology is inexplicable, but he soon became well known for his accurate weather updates. When the city faced its worst rainfall in decades in 2015, he became a guiding light to so many people. That was his internal compass—to give reliable information about the weather to people who can benefit from it. It was something that was uniquely his and made him happy.

Any of the three questions above can help you find your internal compass. Let us take the example of Shashank (from the earlier story) to understand what his What, map, and internal compass were.

His What: To play an important role in his company's growth

The map handed to him: To do a postgraduate degree in marketing

What his compass pointed him towards: To dabble in finance (because of his fascination with numbers)

This, of course, is a minor example, but it shows how there is a difference between mere priorities and those challenges that you wish to solve from your heart. This internal voice from deep within then becomes a part of your internal compass which will guide you to your Why.

In Shashank's case, his compass was internalized from question one (challenges that one wishes to take up) and partly from question two (natural abilities). But the critical takeaway is that for something to become an internal compass, the connection should be strong, and it should originate from our limbic brain—the part of the brain involved in our behavioural and emotional responses. In my story, Shashank kept mentioning how he liked to play with numbers, and how that is where he believed his strength lay.

A lot of people ask me: "If these questions and their answers constitute the internal compass, then how do we find our Why?" The answer is simple, albeit one that needs emphasis and repetition: Our Why arises at the intersection of the three questions mentioned above. Although it may seem that the questions themselves are simple, when you look at them closely, you realize that they require a deeper sense of understanding. Often, you find that you have answers that pertain to only one or two questions among the three. When this happens, it is important to note the fine distinctions, for such answers—although they don't lead us to our Why—still hold implications. Let me explain why. Before we do so, do remember what the three internal-compass questions correspond to:

1. Challenges you learn to take up
2. Natural capability and talent
3. Happiness that comes from within

Innovation

When what comes naturally to you (question 2) also brings forth interesting challenges (question 1) into your life, the result is innovation. However, if there is no joy (question 3) in the process, it still cannot become your Why. The story of a friend of mine, Siva, is a perfect example of this. From childhood, Siva was creative and fond of dabbling in art. When it was time to choose a career, he wanted to pursue a degree in architecture because he was fascinated by the design of different buildings.

However, Siva was forced to pursue a degree in engineering because his parents thought there were few job prospects for an architecture student. Having no say in the matter, he enrolled in a course in Production Engineering. Every semester, during his exams, he complained to his friends about how he didn't want to do the course and would rather do something else with his life. All of us friends could do nothing but empathize with him.

He eventually landed a job in product development. Interestingly, he seemed to have a knack for the job. He performed well and earned a lot of acclaim at work because he was working at tasks that aligned with his strengths. They were also challenging. He was called an innovative performer at his company. Yet, he couldn't find happiness in what he did. The third point of his internal compass—intrinsic joy—was missing. Soon, frustration got to him and he quit. Siva was working at tasks that came naturally to him, and he had the ability to take up those challenges and do well.

In other words, he was an innovator. At the point where talent and challenge merge lies innovation. Yet, what leads to innovation cannot become your Why if it isn't backed by joy or fulfilment.

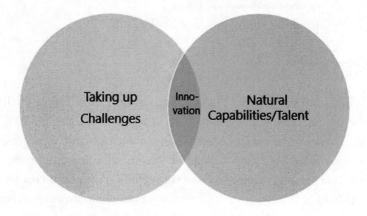

Intuition

On some days, we feel like we are up for a challenge. We may have never done a certain kind of task earlier and not have the talent for it either. Yet we still feel like going ahead anyway. Once it's over, we feel happy about having completed the task. Elated, we try again; only, this time, it doesn't go well. The result doesn't meet our expectations.

I am talking about those tasks that somehow work well the first time but never again. It probably just means that we aren't naturally gifted at them. We decide on those actions intuitively. No one asks us to do them, and often they give us a false sense of pride or overconfidence—if we got them right once, we could do them again, or so we think.

A classic example is that of overconfident businessmen. They play by their own rules because they feel their intuition cannot fail them. In other words, they plunge straight into what they consider as an exciting challenge and what brings them joy. They succeed the first time around. Then, arrogance arrives. They don't evaluate to see if they have the acumen or if they are following the right practices. They go ahead with decisions just because it feels right to them. Well, guess what: it doesn't work and things go south.

This could happen to the best of us sometimes. I don't mean to say that following one's intuition is wrong, but it should almost always be backed by data, capabilities, and clarity of thought. In any case, the fundamental point here is that at the intersection of challenge and happiness lies intuition. However, if intuition is not supported by capability, the process does not lead to our Why.

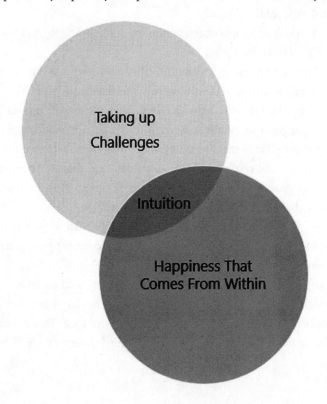

Passion

The other day, I was having a thoughtful conversation about this book with my friend, Sindu. Sindu has been a great source of support and motivation in writing this book. We were discussing how the three questions determine the Why of a person. She pondered for a while and then asked me a question:

"Sagar, I like to read to my grandmother who is quite old now. And I think I do a fairly good job at it. I also feel a tremendous amount of happiness while doing it. So, if I like what I do and I am using a strength of mine, can't this activity be my Why? I would certainly like it to be. It is one of my favourite things in the world to do!" she said.

As much as I appreciated where she was coming from, I had to disagree. I explained why:

"Interesting thought, Sindu! But you are missing a key characteristic of the triad: the 'solving the challenges' part. Yes, you are using your talent and you derive happiness from it. It is, in this case, your passion. At the intersection of capability and happiness lies passion. But it still doesn't become your Why because you are not solving any challenge here. Activities that you are passionate about get you through difficult times. But unless they are used to solve a challenge, they cannot become your Why."

To better understand my answer, imagine an artist working at something he is passionate about for his own happiness, using his natural capability. It still doesn't become his Why because he doesn't solve any challenges. "What challenges could an artist solve through his art?" you may ask. Well, perhaps he may want to rouse emotion for a cause or nurture an impactful idea. When artists dedicate their life to this kind of purpose, it becomes their 'Why.'

I agree with those who say that when you turn your passion into a business, you live life to the fullest. This is because it naturally becomes your Why. As Simon Sinek says—the work you do, or the passion you have, should solve problems, and at the same time, be something that you wouldn't mind doing for free. That is why at the intersection of these three questions, you find your Why.

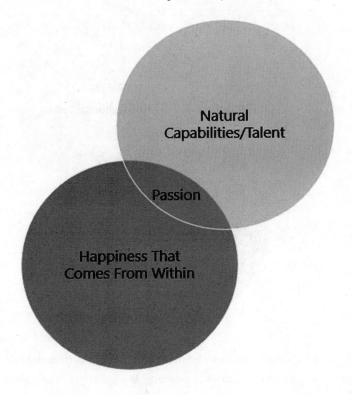

The Pursuit of Your Why

When you combine the power of your passion, your ability to innovate, and your intuition, you get your Why.

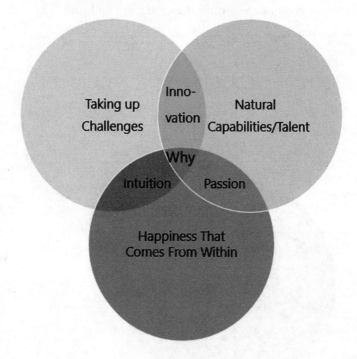

It is important that you constantly look for signs to understand what your internal compass is pointing at so that you can ground all your decisions on meaningful factors rather than just money, success, or social validation. When you start to align your activities with your internal compass, they become so much more powerful. They become a part of your purpose in life.

Having a true sense of Why at everything you do is a journey and a truly long one.

You will now do an exercise that will help you chart your compass. You will write down the priorities that you mentioned earlier in the chapter. As you know well by now, these are your Whats. In the Map column, write down what you have been conditioned to think, albeit in an unconstructive autopilot manner, with respect to each What. And if you look closely, every priority has a reason behind it—some strong and some not so much. This becomes your compass.

Below, I chart my compass to the Whats I had mentioned earlier:

What	My Map	My Compass
Add at least two major customers to our portfolio in the next six months.	Get in touch with customers and wait for them to respond.	Use my contacts and communication skills to develop a rapport with customers because that is where my strength lies. (Example of Innovation)
Make sure that I spend enough time with my wife, Devangee, and give enough care in the upbringing of my son, Aarav.	Work at least seventy hours a week. Never take a break.	Spend quality time with my family despite having a busy schedule because it gives me happiness. (Example of Passion)
Make sure I finish writing this book and publish it before the end of 2022	Believe that if one hasn't written a book before, it will be a long and arduous task.	Prioritize finishing my book, overcoming any challenges that may come because I refuse to be deterred. (Example of Intuition)

In the chart above, I have mentioned each reason in the Compass column as an example of passion, intuition, or innovation. This is only so that you get an idea of how a variable can be split and understood in terms of these three parameters. It is not necessary that you do the same.

Why don't you now quickly derive your compass from your What in the table below. Try to understand the maps that have ruled your thoughts and then chart out the compass.

Your compass should contain things that bring you happiness, things that you automatically want to do, and wherever possible, things that you are uniquely suited for. If you can't find something that resonates with any of these three points, I suggest that you leave those spaces blank. We will look at how to deal with them later.

(People usually ask me this question while learning about maps and compasses: "Can the map handed to me also act as my compass?" The answer is yes. Like I said earlier, some people can find their way with others' maps. But it is important that you make that experience your own and then decide if it acts as your compass.)

What	Your Map	Your Compass

The first question I want to ask once you have filled the table is if you left any field blank in the Compass column.

This usually happens when your What is not aligned with your compass; when you do something just for the sake of it. This doesn't mean you shouldn't do it. Sometimes, this is also necessary. There are people unhappy with their job, but they continue to work at it because it's the source of their livelihood. Financial security is important to most of us. But at the same time, look at how you can move out of these Whats and focus on a What that gives you happiness in the long term—things connected to your compass.

> **"Trust your own instinct. Your mistakes might as well be your own, instead of someone else's!"**
>
> *Billy Wilder*

Let us now quickly recap all that we learned in this chapter, shall we? Your purpose is made up of two components: your What and your Why. Your Why makes your What powerful and is usually derived from your limbic brain. Your What is made up of your priorities—activities that you perform on a daily basis. You will always do a few tasks just for the sake of it, which will make life less fulfilling. Therefore, it is important for you to find your internal compass. Your compass consists of whatever makes you happy, whatever you are naturally good at, and whatever you want to do instinctively. When you find something that meets all three criteria, it guides you to your Why.

Naturally, finding your Why is a challenge, but it is a challenge that will provide you with clarity. Life can be perceived in many ways, but there's one constant: challenges and adversities. Facing these with a lot of grit will help you grow into a better, stronger human being. You may feel crippled by some of these adversities, while others you might manage well. But at the end of the day, all adversities teach you something. The real question is, are you listening? Are you aware of what they are teaching you?

Being self-aware is a gift. If you choose to ignore that gift, you may lead a delusional life. And if you choose to embrace the beauty and ridiculousness of this gift, you will get an illuminating sense of clarity. This clarity is the first step to feeling fulfilled. To get on that journey of self-awareness, you need to have an absurd amount of belief, clarity in thought, and a tremendous amount of courage. I hope that as you proceed through the chapters of this book, you manage to find all of these.

Chapter Summary

- Purpose is the reason why something is created or accomplished and the pursuit of it is never ending.
- Purpose = (What) ^ (Why)
- Your 'What' comes from your priorities.
- To get to know your 'Why' you need to follow your internal compass.
- When you try to connect your priorities to your internal compass, they become much more powerful.
- Your internal compass can be found by answering three questions:
- What challenges do you pursue that others are afraid to take up?
- What comes naturally to you?
- What makes you happy even though you can't explain why?
- When you combine the power of your passion, your ability to innovate, and your intuition, you get your 'Why'.
- Being self-aware is a gift that can liberate you.

C H A P T E R

3

Bringing Your Priorities to Life

"Align your core to your priorities and
everything else will start to fall in place."

Sagar Makwana

Your Core Is Who You Are!

An understanding of your purpose is only the beginning as you start to paint the canvas called life. It is important that you also understand how you can bring your priorities to life. The most powerful tool at your disposal while working on your priorities is simple: yourself. Before we discuss this idea further, we will read a short story about a bunch of friends in college. It's a story about friendship, differences, and good times. It's also a story about knowing that there's more to life than what meets the eye.

Venky, Raju, Satty, Pipe (yes, one of them is called Pipe), Siva, Karthi, Nagappa, and Sam—these were my good friends in college, and all of us stayed together in the college hostel.

The middle of the night is the busiest time in a hostel. You will find lovers talking to each other on the phone, friends having random jam sessions, a dozen youngsters crammed in a room meant for two just so that they can watch the latest movies together, Counterstrike/COD matches being played between people in adjacent rooms, friends having a drink together, a few sharing a smoke, and the most peace-loving folks getting high with a joint, with the innocent ones having fun watching them.

This story, however, happened on a night that's quite unlike what I just described because the next day, we were going to face one of the toughest exams of our lives. Those of you who have lived in a hostel, I am sure you remember the night before the final semester exams. There's chaos. There's calm. And there's chaos in the calm. The subject was fluid mechanics, taught by the head of the department, Dr. Velu, and we knew it wasn't going to be easy. To top it all, he strongly disliked most of us (except Pipe).

It was a quarter past twelve. Siva had given up studying by ten and was already dozing off in his room. Raju was mugging up the important concepts and mathematical problems. He didn't have the time to understand them.

"What if they interchange the numbers in the exam?" Sam asked Raju.

Raju, holding a cigarette in his hand, coolly remarked, "Don't worry, *machi* (slang for 'pal'), I am mugging up the numbers too. If I realize that the numbers have been changed, I will just look at what Satty is writing and copy it."

Nagappa was sitting in his room, just about to finish watching a movie. "I can't be stressed while I study. This will help me relax and then I will be as fresh as ever. I have a plan," he told Pipe in a zen-like manner. By the time the movie was about to get over, Pipe knew that it was time to slip away.

Pipe absconded. Everyone knew that he was completing his tenth revision somewhere in peace. He knew that if he came anywhere near us, we would ask him to explain a concept, and then another, until it was time for the exam. He was that guy who had copies of all the old question papers, along with their answers. "According to the law of averages, Velu is bound to ask us this concept this time!" he would remark, not knowing that we couldn't care less.

Venky, Satty, and Karthi were having a group study session, desperately trying to understand the concepts. Karthi was already frustrated.

"Let's go to the snack bar, eat something, and then start afresh," he suggested.

"It is the end of the semester, we have a lot to study, and more importantly, I don't have money da!" Venky said.

"This one's on me, let's just go. I can't sit here anymore!" Karthi said. Venky hugged him. Wasn't this guy the sweetest!

An hour later, the three were back at it but were nowhere close to understanding anything. "Desperate times need desperate measures," they thought. It was time to go to the one person who had finished studying and was just about to sleep—Sam! There was one problem though: Sam had his own peculiar ways of understanding concepts—sometimes leading to more confusion. But they were willing to take a risk; there was no other way.

They begged Sam to teach them something, but he wanted to sleep. After a few attempts at emotional blackmail, Sam agreed.

Sam started talking to them about pneumatics, air hoses, cylinders, solenoids, valves, and whatnot.

"So when you force air with pressure through this valve, and when the valve is in this position, the air comes out from here at a pressure of . . ." Sam went on and on. Until Venky stopped him.

"Wait. You say that the air goes from this point to that one. But how does that happen?" he asked.

"The force from the place here goes here and then this happens. Got it?" Sam blabbered. In all honesty, he didn't know what he was saying anymore. But it was a matter of pride. "If you can't convince them, confuse them!" he thought.

"But how exactly does that happen?" Venky persisted.

"It happens because . . . It's . . . It's . . . IT'S PNEUMATICS DA!" Sam said. There was a confused look on everyone's face now.

"Okay, so you got this. Great! I am going to sleep now. I am tired. Plus, I need to wake up to have breakfast on time. Good night, buddies." Sam left and went to his room. Venky was more confused than he had been earlier.

It wasn't until the next morning, when Pipe taught Venky the same concept that Sam had explained the previous night, that he realized that Sam didn't know what he was talking about. A few minutes later, Sam woke up to the sound of a slipper slapping his bum. It was Venky and he was furious. Everyone else around was laughing.

It has been twelve years since that incident occurred, and we still laugh each time we think of it. When we don't want to explain something (or simply don't know how to explain something), we just say, "IT'S PNEUMATICS DA!"

These wonderful characters have been my strength right from the first day of college. We have had our share of good times and tough times, wins and losses, inspiration and failure, joy and sadness, love and strife. There has never been a moment when we weren't there for each other.

What life in college primarily taught me is that each of us is built differently and it is important to embrace all of this. All of us have our strengths and weaknesses, and this makes us who we are. Once we understand our priorities, we need to embrace something important: ourselves.

Embrace the uniqueness of yourself and others.

All of us have a set of preferences, strengths, and ideas that become an integral part of who we are, and it is usually difficult to change them. Our priorities and purpose can be fulfilled only when it is aligned to our core values.

Let's say you want to join the army, but you have a tendency to procrastinate and are usually late to meetings. You may still join the army, but it will become difficult for you to get in line with the standards set there. A knowledge of ourselves can help us inculcate new values or align our priorities better to our core strengths. Let us first understand the broad categories of core strengths.

The Four Core Strengths and What They Mean

I like to ask questions—and I often end up asking a lot of questions in any situation. I believe that curiosity helps us cultivate an open mind and understand better the people we meet from myriad walks of life. Curiosity and an open mind are also terrific assets in the coaching and mentoring business. Over the course of several coaching sessions, I have come to realize that people live with a few important characteristics in their lives, which makes them who they are. I like to call them core strengths. A core strength is any quality that helps navigate the journey toward realizing one's potential effortlessly. There are many traits that can be regarded as comprising the core strength of a person—traits such as health, self-love, passion, and belief. But for the sake of simplicity and effectiveness, we will consider four primary core strengths: time, money, relationships, and ambition. All other factors that may appear as strengths manifest from these four values that we will talk about. Whoever we are or whatever we become is usually a by-product of these four core areas.

Time

> **"The mark of a great man is one who knows
> when to set aside the important things
> in order to accomplish the vital ones."**

> *Brandon Sanderson*

Time—a valuable resource that can only be spent and not stored. What I mean by time here isn't particularly time management, and you will see why in chapter eight. Your core challenge with respect to time is how you value it and make it your ally. It is how you spend your time that makes a profound impact on your life rather than how you believe you manage it. Therefore, we will talk about 'Priorities Enhancement' instead of time management. Just as the quote above mentions, I believe that time can become your core strength when you understand how to utilize it best for things that matter to you.

All successful people apply this simple concept in their lives. They always plan their activities for the day and sometimes plan their priorities months in advance. They stick to a schedule to be as effective as possible. I want to quote the noteworthy ancient philosopher Lao Tzu here:

> **"Time is a created thing. To say 'I don't have time' is like saying 'I don't want to.'"**

I don't think I can talk in a paragraph or two about how time is the most important of all core strengths. So I've dedicated a whole chapter to it. But do understand that whatever you do today, at this moment, including reading this book, can influence how you can accomplish your priorities.

Money

> **"Money is a terrible master but an excellent servant."**
>
> *P.T. Barnum*

Attitude towards money is relative—rich people sometimes think they don't have enough, while people with less think that they have more than enough. That's why money as a core concept is a bit confusing. How do you determine the worth of money when there is no one way to understand its importance? I believe that money by itself isn't the core strength. It is how you handle your money that determines how money works as a core strength for you. While you do know that money is just a part of the flow of life, there needs to be a clear understanding of how you work with money.

There is no right or wrong way to handle money, but understanding its importance and how it can affect your priorities is crucial. People who believe money to be just another factor in their lives sometimes have more control over it than those who don't.

Relationships

> **"Relationships don't always make sense. Especially from the outside."**

> *Sarah Dessen, Along for the Ride*

An important aspect of life for most people, relationships can often make or break someone. The right relationship can push you to become a better person in every way possible, whereas a wrong relationship may ruin you. When I talk about relationships, it is not limited to those with your mother, father, spouse, and siblings. Relationships even with your friends, cousins, and other close and distant members can determine what your core is. How you build a social circle around yourself and, in turn, how it influences you goes a long way in determining your growth and priorities.

Despite all of this, the most important relationship that you will ever have is the one you hold with yourself. Always remember that through introspection arises an understanding of the self. Through self-understanding comes self-esteem, and from self-esteem comes self-confidence. From self-confidence stems self-belief. And from self-confidence also arises your ability to reach for the stars.

A healthy relationship builds the ability to love oneself and others, and I believe love is the second-best medicine one can receive (laughter still retains the top spot). Jokes apart, people surrounded by several healthy relationships are way happier than those who aren't, irrespective of their financial or social position.

Ambition

"Ambition is enthusiasm with a purpose."

Frank Tyger

I believe ambition is the most personal of all the core strengths. This is because ambition is something that spurts from within. Yes, external factors will determine how things work for you, but you can't take away the core of a person. For example, a person can be ambitious about how she leads her team at work or how she runs her business. An ambitious person is usually someone who aims high and holds themselves or others to unrealistic expectations. But when channelled in the right manner, this drive can help create magical, fulfilling, and transformative journeys.

Ambition buffers a person's thoughts and beliefs against challenges, and I believe that being ambitious can never go wrong unless it is poisoned by ego. The best example of this kind of person is Vijay Mallya, who had a unique and enviable sense of business acumen, until one day, when he woke up and started to think he was invincible. His ego and pride started to rule his ambitions and the rest is history.

Self-assessment

How about we assess your core strengths now? What comes naturally to you? Does your ability shine through with respect to time, money, relationships, or ambition? Here is a short test for you to find out, but first, a few important instructions to note:

Whenever I fill up any assessment form, I first look at all the questions and their answer options. Then I try to analyse how the questionnaire will be assessed. Finally, I answer the questions in a manner that suits me—making me look good to the assessor and, probably, to myself, as well. Guess what—this is exactly how I do NOT want you to take this assessment. If you are anything like me, then you need to pause. Take a deep breath. Understand that whatever bubble you live in that makes you think that you must look good, even to yourself, is a farce. It is time now to move on. Follow these simple rules when answering the questions:

1. Don't look at all the sections at the beginning itself.
2. Proceed in order, from the first section to the second, and so on.
3. Don't skip sections.
4. While reading the questions, try to imagine yourself in the corresponding situations and think of what you would have most likely done.

As already mentioned, we are going to concentrate on the four core principles so as to understand what values and principles determine the pursuit of your priorities.

1. Time

a. Are you a procrastinator or do you finish work earlier than required?

☐ I procrastinate a LOT!

☐ I try not to procrastinate but still end up doing so.

☐ Even if I procrastinate, I manage to finish my work on time, thanks to the last-minute hustle.

☐ I am usually (but not always) ahead of my tasks.

☐ My planning can never go wrong!

b. Are you almost always on time everywhere or do people usually crib about you being late?

☐ I get out of bed a few minutes before a scheduled meeting.

☐ I somehow end up getting late for my appointments, and people hate that about me.

☐ I make an effort to be on time, but I am usually fifteen-twenty minutes late.

☐ I am almost always on time.

☐ I arrive for a meeting at least fifteen mins before the scheduled time.

c. Do you start your day with a list of planned activities?

☐ No way! I will do what I want to do, whenever I want to do it.

☐ I let the day's flow decide my schedule.

☐ I think about the most important tasks for the day and prioritize them.

☐ I know what I need to do, but I don't usually note it down.

☐ I never go anywhere without my planner!

d. At the end of the day, do you analyse if you were able to focus on your priorities?

- ☐ No, I couldn't care less.
- ☐ Life is about living in the moment, so I think a little about the day but not much.
- ☐ I try to understand how I could have avoided wasting time on any day.
- ☐ I analyse every hour and plan my time meticulously.
- ☐ I can show you data to support how I analyse my time!

e. Do you have the courage to say no to a task when you don't have the time to do it?

- ☐ I am a people pleaser. I simply can't say no.
- ☐ Even though I try hard to say no, I still end up doing what I don't want to do.
- ☐ I can sometimes say no, but not always.
- ☐ I take up a task only if I feel like it.
- ☐ I focus only on my priorities and what I like to do.

2. Money

a. Do you save a lot of what you earn?

- ☐ Regardless of how much I earn, I save most of it.
- ☐ I calculate my expenses and usually plan to save more than what is possible at present.
- ☐ I save more if I earn more. My expenses don't go down.
- ☐ I save a little, but it doesn't last for long.
- ☐ Savings? What savings? Money is earned to be spent!

b. When a friend asks you to lend money (and it doesn't seem like a genuine cause), and you can afford to do so, what do you do?

☐ Only in rare cases do I lend money to someone.

☐ If I am 100% sure that I will get back my money, I will lend it.

☐ I will look at how the favour will benefit me before deciding to give money.

☐ If they persistently ask, I may end up giving them the money.

☐ It doesn't matter who asks. If I have the money, I give it, without expecting it back.

c. You feel the need to buy something expensive and a little out of your budget. What do you do?

☐ If something is out of my budget, there is no way I am thinking about it.

☐ I assess my income and see if I can squeeze my budget a little so that I can buy what I want.

☐ I tend to look for means to justify my purchase and then go for it.

☐ If it is something I badly want, it is difficult for me to control my impulse.

☐ Things that are out of my budget? My house is filled with that stuff!

d. When you go out for dinner with friends, do you like to split the bill?

☐ I don't prefer splitting the bill. I want to pay only for what I eat.

☐ I am okay with splitting the bill. Since I usually

end up eating a lot more than the others, it's advantageous for me.

☐ Splitting the bill is the best option there is.

☐ If there are just three or four of us, then I prefer to pay.

☐ Regardless of the number of people, dinner is usually on me!

e. How do you decide if you want to donate money to a fundraiser?

☐ If I have extra money that month after all the necessary expenditures, then I will donate.

☐ If it is a cause that holds personal significance, I will donate.

☐ If I see that a friend has donated some money to the cause, I will do so too.

☐ If the fundraiser's message appeals to me, I will donate.

☐ It doesn't matter what the charity is. I will donate anyway to my best possible means.

3. Relationships

a. Do you manage to maintain cordial relationships with everyone around you?

☐ Would a loner care about the people around him?

☐ I don't care much about who holds a good relationship with me.

☐ I invest a little effort to maintain cordial relationships.

☐ I sometimes go out of my way to get someone to like me.

☐ People around me usually like me because I always put an effort to maintain every relationship I have!

b. Do you get easily influenced by the people close to you?

☐ Never in my wildest dreams can someone influence me.

☐ I value my own opinion the most.

☐ I will consider others' opinions, but I usually do what I want to do.

☐ I hear everyone out and then follow the advice I like the most.

☐ I usually like others to lead the way.

c. Do you allow other people's priorities and ideas to affect how you make decisions?

☐ I am what I am because I stopped caring about others a long time ago.

☐ My feelings hold the most importance, but I may consider the views of people who are close to me.

☐ If it doesn't affect me much, I may consider others' priorities.

☐ It is important for me to know that my decisions won't affect others in any way.

☐ I mostly make decisions based on how others will react to it or get affected by it.

d. **Would you rather spend time by yourself or with a bunch of friends on a free evening?**

   ☐ Born alone, live alone, die alone. That's my motto.

   ☐ I can handle one or two people around me at the most.

   ☐ Sometimes I socialize well.

   ☐ I usually like to have company over often.

   ☐ If I don't have people around me, I go crazy.

e. **Your friends decide to have a house party. What do you decide to do?**

   ☐ I don't care where the party is because I ain't going!

   ☐ Why bother with a house party? Let's just go to a bar or restaurant.

   ☐ I don't mind going to a party as long as it is not at my place!

   ☐ I like to have parties at home, but only occasionally.

   ☐ It's always party time at my place. My homies hang out at my place every night!

4. **Ambition**

a. **Are you a go-getter or a happy-go-lucky person?**

   ☐ I believe in the flow of life: whatever has to happen will happen, whether I make an effort or not.

   ☐ I pretty much don't care where my career or life takes me.

   ☐ Goals are not everything for me. But I do like to assess myself once in a while.

   ☐ Targets, targets, and more targets. I like to set them and achieve them.

   ☐ My dreams are everything and I will stop nowhere before I achieve them.

b. Do you feel like pushing your limits often?

- ☐ I like to stay in my comfort zone.
- ☐ I like to push my limits occasionally.
- ☐ I plan to get out of my comfort zone slowly but surely.
- ☐ I like to take on challenges once in a while to test myself.
- ☐ My day starts and ends with challenges and I usually succeed in overcoming them.

c. Do you believe in dreams or in being grounded in reality?

- ☐ At any point, I want to know what I am doing and how it will affect my life.
- ☐ I sometimes wish I had more freedom but I am unable to let go of things weighing me down.
- ☐ I dare to dream but just a little.
- ☐ I don't like being held back by anything.
- ☐ I don't need Redbull to give me wings. I was born with them!

d. How do you feel when taking risks?

- ☐ I don't take risks with money or other important aspects of my life. 'Play Small, Play Safe' is my motto.
- ☐ I take a risk only when I know I am in complete control.
- ☐ Calculated risks should be taken sometimes.
- ☐ I like to play the high risk, high reward game sometimes but not always.
- ☐ 'No risk, no life.' I like to live life like there's no tomorrow.

e. Once you set a goal for yourself, how do you pursue it?

☐ I set goals, I get bored, and then I set new goals.

☐ I set goals and create a plan but if the going gets tough, I stop.

☐ I take a sincere approach to my goals and don't bend down to challenges.

☐ I rarely lose sight of what I want to achieve.

☐ If I decide to do something, I won't stop until I achieve it.

Let us now get to the results of your assessment. The scoring pattern is simple. The first option in every question carries 1 point, the second option 2 points, and so on. For example, the options of the first question (Q1) of the Time section can be graded in the following manner:

1. Point: I procrastinate A LOT!
2. Points: I try not to procrastinate but still end up doing so.
3. Points: Even if I procrastinate, I manage to finish my work on time, thanks to the last-minute hustle.
4. Points: I am usually (but not always) ahead of my tasks.
5. Points: My planning can never go wrong!

In a similar manner, note down in the table below the points you have scored for all the questions in the four sections. For each of the four core strength variables, add the total and divide the number by five. This is your score for that core strength.

Core Area	Points					Total	Average (Total/5)
	Q1	Q2	Q3	Q4	Q5		
Time							
Money							
Relationships							
Ambition							

Now that you know your scores, it is time to analyse them.

From my observations in doing this exercise with several people, I find that if one's score for a core strength is 3 or more, then it becomes their dominant core. Usually, it is unlikely to have more than three dominant core strengths. In other words, at least one of your core areas will have a score of less than 3. If you find that all your scores are above 3, I request you to take the test again carefully, pausing to think if you are being true to yourself.

Let us now understand what your scores mean.

How Your Core Dictates
the Happenings of Your Life

Time: If you scored high on time, you value your priorities highly and plan your day well. This means that when you are out to achieve something, you plan for it well and also stick to your plan. As I said earlier, time (I also like to call it 'priorities enhancement') is one of the more important cores among the four, simply because it becomes a key factor in determining the type of returns you get in life, which we will talk about in the next chapter.

As someone with a high time score, I am sometimes jealous of people with lower scores because their life seems to run smoothly: they are able to live life in a less rigid manner, thus getting less stressed on a daily basis. I agree that not every priority needs to be time-sensitive, and some of the most creative people in the world don't believe in being constrained by time. And yet, clichéd as it may sound, I believe that since we all have limited time in our lives, it helps to have some clarity on how our priorities should be paced through the day, week, or month.

A low score indicates that you don't always obsess over things being a certain way. Does that go against understanding your priorities and working towards them? Sometimes, yes. It could also lead one to become lethargic, but the beauty of life is such that you can't always claim one approach is better than the other. Because people who are flexible with their time also have the capacity to create with their hearts and not get bogged down by the usual target-setting, over-achieving attitude that has become quite the norm in today's world.

Among my friends (whom you got fairly acquainted with at the beginning of the chapter), Sam and Pipe have a high time score. These were the guys who used to finish studying way ahead of the examination and only had to review their notes before the big day. They knew and understood what their priorities were and stuck to them.

Money: This is a tricky one among the core values: people believe that if their money score is high, then they have good money management skills. But this test doesn't measure your ability to make or manage money, but rather how ready you are to part with money. Yes! If your money score is high, then it means that you are relatively less stringent on a daily basis about where your money gets spent. You do not account for every penny or allot it to a particular category in advance. You are flexible in the short term about spending money, although you may (or may not) have good long-term plans. A high money score means that you are quite okay to spend on what isn't necessarily important but brings joy regardless.

You may or may not be good at financial management, but if your money score is high in this test, excess money doesn't stay with you for a long time. You end up spending it or giving it away. Why does this trait get a high score even though it sounds undesirable? Because sometimes it is a good thing! You will see why in the next chapter.

If your money score is low, it means that you value wealth highly and can't let go of it easily. Sometimes, this comes at a cost—you let go of relationships to hold on to your money. On the upside, your financial planning is on point.

To sum up, having a low score or a high score, both have their pros and cons. People who save more and are stringent with their money, cruise through life more easily simply because they make sure they have enough before spending it on things that aren't an absolute necessity. Whereas people who don't believe in restricting their outflow of money, tend to be more liked. But they are the ones who usually get into trouble because of a lack of discipline.

Among my friends, there are two who have never thought about money as a priority or a deterrent. They are Raju and Nagappa. They believe that money is just another aspect of their lives and spend it on whatever or whoever they want to spend it on.

Relationships: There are three ways to infer the relationship score. First, if your relationship score is high, it means that you are more a giver than a taker in your relationships. You are a generous person, and it is important for you to be liked by the people around you. If you scored between 2 and 3, you are likely someone who stays in stable, mutually fulfilling relationships, and you believe in the power of collaboration and love. A low score points at a cautious outlook toward people. You prioritize yourself over others. We will not debate whether this is a good thing or not. Afterall, when we talk about relationships, we need to include our relationship with ourselves too.

When it comes to relationships, Venkat, Karthi, and Siva are my friends who are always warm and loving. They always put others ahead of themselves, which is why people love them (and sometimes take advantage of them too).

Ambition: This core strength, I believe, is the hardest to balance. Most people feel the need to be ambitious because of the way they have been conditioned since childhood. It takes a long time to understand whether being ambitious is our core strength or a mere conditioning. But the sooner we understand it, the better.

If your ambition score is high, it means that you are willing to take risks. You expect higher rewards for your efforts, and higher rewards come bundled with higher risks. When the Wright brothers set out to build the first airplane in the world, they were aware that they could fail miserably, but that didn't deter them from building it.

I do feel that there is one small concern in being highly ambitious—it can lead to a false sense of security. An example I can think of is Harshad Mehta, the infamous stockbroker who took the

Indian stock market by storm back in the early '90s. At one point, he had an enviable amount of money and a wonderful reputation. He could have lived the rest of his life in peace with what he had accomplished in just a few years. But he started to believe he was invincible and that pretty much led to his downfall. He took pride in that downfall too! He went down fighting and even made some sensational claims against the Government of India.

Then there's the other end of it—being less ambitious. If this is the case, you sometimes compromise on your thoughts, values, and priorities. You tag along with someone else's dreams and values, limiting your opportunities. The sooner you get out of this rut, the better.

Among my friends, there are two who believe in their vision and always try to look for the next goal to work with: Sathya and Sam. They never back down from a challenge; getting ahead in life is the most important thing to them.

Other Conclusions

A lot of people ask me why I haven't included health as a core strength. This is because health is a by-product of relationships and ambition. If you believe in having a strong relationship with yourself and your body, then health will inevitably become a strong priority. Similarly, you can be ambitious in how you set your health-based targets.

Another pertinent question that arises is, "Why can't someone be dominant in all the four core strengths since all of them seem important?" Well, this is difficult because life is a huge balancing act by itself, and it is quite difficult to juggle all areas well. A small number of people do get a score of 3 or more in all the core areas. But it could also mean that they are playing a dangerous game and that their priorities and purpose are all over the place.

Further, some cores directly oppose each other. Scores on time and money, for instance, are usually inversely proportional to each other. A person who gives a lot of importance to time will find it difficult to easily let go of money. Such people tend to subconsciously relate time with money. Some of you may disagree with this but do observe the people around you closely, and you will tend to notice that people who have strict principles about how they manage their time and priorities will also have strict principles about how they spend money. My father was a principled man, and he was clear about his opinions, ideas, and time. Naturally, he guarded his money well. This doesn't mean he didn't donate to charity or take care of his family. It just means that he valued money a lot and wouldn't spend it on things that didn't seem worth it.

Relationships and ambition hold a similar relationship. A person who gives a lot to their relationships will usually tend to compromise on their ambition and vice versa. Some people call it unfair, but it is what it is. I am sure you must have observed a few people around you who seem to be so engrossed in their work that they don't seem to have time even for their most important relationships. One of my friends was this way, and it naturally put a lot of strain on his marriage. His spouse was also focussed on her career in marketing, and it sometimes felt like they lived in two different worlds. Therefore, for relationships to bloom, ambition may have to take a backseat at times. This doesn't mean you don't honour your ambition but that you have to evaluate your priorities time and again.

Aligning Your Core to Your Priorities

Now that you are aware of your dominant core strengths, let us understand how you can use them to better realize your priorities (which you listed in chapter two) and solve the challenges around achieving them.

There needs to be a direct correlation between your priorities and your core. For example, if your priority is to double the growth of your business in the next two years, then you need to have a strong core in time and ambition. If your priority is to have a strong relationship with yourself and your spouse, then you need to have a strong relationship core. Awareness is important here; I can't emphasize enough the importance of awareness.

**Align your core to your priorities and
everything else will start to fall in place.**

Let's now do a short exercise to see how well our core aligns to our priorities. I have stated below one of my priorities and the corresponding core strengths required to realize it.

My Priorities	Core Strengths Required
Create training programs to help people develop greater awareness of their abilities.	Time and Ambition (In short, it is important that I stick to a plan, prepare to face failure, and take risks.)

Why don't you now fill the table below with your priorities (as mentioned in the previous chapter) and the corresponding core strengths that you believe they require?

My Priorities	Core Strengths Required

This exercise naturally leads to a disconcerting question: What if my core and priorities aren't in alignment? Well, it is certainly possible. In fact, it may be the case that your core strengths don't support your priorities at all. What do you do in that case?

To explain that, I am going to talk about my friend Siva again.

As you read in the previous chapter, Siva never wanted to pursue a degree in engineering, and it took him a long time to accept that he was not going to find happiness in it. After finishing his degree, he went on to work for a good firm but he still couldn't find happiness at what he did. One day, he decided that enough was enough and that his priorities lay elsewhere. If he wanted to chase his dreams, he would have to take a risk, quit his job, and try to pursue a degree in design.

The problem, however, was that he had never been ambitious. It was difficult for him to take the risk involved in a career change. Moreover, he wasn't in a sound position financially. Siva knew that if he quit his job, he wouldn't have much time before he would have to start earning again. And yet, despite all that, Siva was determined.

It took a while for him to build his ambition core, and slowly but surely, with the help of his parents and friends, he mustered the courage to quit his job. He went on to do his master's degree in an institute in Pune. His perseverance and creativity brought him a lot of accolades.

A few years have passed since and Siva now works for one of India's largest design firms. He is also a design-thinking expert and consultant. Had he given in to his natural tendency, Siva would still be a miserable engineer working in some company, cursing his boss for what he was being asked to do every day. He would have hated his life and never turned out to be the free-spirited, insightful person that he is today. Sometimes, you have to make a choice. If your core is not aligned to your priorities, you need to reshape your core—sans excuse, self-pity, or complaints. Wondering how to do that? Just focus on the qualities outlined in the assessment. Let me elaborate.

Reshaping Your Core Strengths

Our core, often built and fortified over several years, does not easily yield to change. The first step toward improving a core strength is wanting to improve it—and wanting it badly. You must be utterly convinced that change can happen, and your priorities will come alive only if you undo old patterns of thought and forge new habits and behaviour. Change is hard, and your mind will throw several excuses at you to convince you to give up, but this can be prevented to a large extent by a strong sense of conviction.

Apart from conviction, there are other important factors that will guide you on your journey: patience, consistency, persistence, and rigour.

Time

If you are someone who has never planned for a day much in advance, doing so suddenly may seem like a huge uphill task but the key is to approach it in increments. Commit to a single task for the next day, to begin with. As you consistently begin to finish planned tasks day after day, you will slowly get into the groove of planning much bigger chunks of time in advance. Be patient and don't aim for the stars immediately. More importantly, it's okay if you fail or miss a few days. Simply start again.

The same goes for quitting the habit of procrastinating. Start small. Make it a point to spend at least ten minutes on a task as soon as you commit to it. Having put in a small amount of effort will bring you back to the task quicker than is usually the case. Eventually, you will get to a place where you don't hesitate to tackle any job at the earliest rather than keep it for later.

You could, of course, also want to go the other way: perhaps you are too rigid with your time and that is hurting you in areas of your life that require a little flexibility. In that case, you can try to ease a bit, plan less, and go with the flow.

Money

With money, there are always going to be varying notions of what the right approach constitutes. Money is a subjective topic, so it is important that one first understands their spending patterns to see if they want to be more careful with spending their money. Self-knowledge goes a long way with this core strength.

Self-knowledge is also crucial to introspect the reasons behind a low score in this strength. What drives you to be stringent about spending money? Is it fear? Insecurity? Are these well founded or can they be addressed?

At the other end, if one's pattern of spending money is out of control, then they need to take a long and hard look at how impulse buying is affecting their life and how they can better integrate prudent financial planning in their lives. All of this needs a patient and yet rigorous approach.

Relationships

Perhaps the area that requires the most patience is relationships. While handling relationships, it is important to introspect if you are giving more than what you are taking from a relationship, and if this may hurt you in the long run. In that case, you need to start looking at how you can stop letting others influence your decisions and how you can learn to say no to what you aren't going to put up with.

On the other hand, if you feel that you are too lonely or want to forge more healthy relationships with the people around you, perhaps you can try to venture a little out of your comfort zone. It is not necessary to be liked by everyone but meaningful connections are a huge source of joy, aren't they?

Ambition

In the case of ambition, it is easy to fall toward one of the extremes, by being either too ambitious or too cautious. In the latter scenario, we tend to not challenge ourselves and that could create a vacuum in our life. As with the case of Siva, if you are less ambitious, you may get stuck in a job or situation that doesn't fulfil you. Sometimes it is worth the risk to take a leap of faith and do better things with your time.

At the same time, being too ambitious can also be risky as pride takes over and you tend to think of yourself as invincible.

As much as some self-help gurus will tell you that this is the right way to go, it is important that you draw the curtain of reality sometimes.

All of this does sound simple on paper but the challenge, as I mentioned earlier, lies in being rigorous and consistent. Just as how a six-pack core can be developed only through an immense amount of effort and repetition, your core strengths are also cultivated only when you work on them every day with determination.

After all, that is what First Principles Thinking has taught us. You know what your priorities are. You know what your core should be to accomplish them. So now work on it. Everything else is just an assumption.

The Way Ahead

At this point, if you still feel a bit unsure of how to go about all this, worry not. You will learn more about the four core areas in the forthcoming chapters—how they influence your life, what factors shape them, and how you can build a better core so that you can achieve your priorities the way you want to.

Having clarity over how your core values align with your priorities solves any major concerns that arise when working outside your comfort zone.

The biggest tool that you hold right now to achieve your priorities is your core. Your path to achieving your priorities may change, the people around you may change, and your priorities themselves may change. But what will never change is your ability to work on yourself according to your priorities.

You need to understand this: unless you make a sincere effort to empower yourself and strengthen your core, you will end up running in the wrong direction. And when you lose your sense of direction, you lose your sense of fulfilment along with it.

We talked about priorities in the last chapter. We now understand how our core can influence us and provide a path to achieving our priorities. But then the question remains: What do our priorities bring in return? Shouldn't we ideally be getting something in return for all the efforts we take to develop our core and work towards our priorities? Of course, we should. And this is what the next chapter discusses.

Chapter Summary

- All of us have our own strengths and weaknesses that are integral to us and it is usually difficult to change them.
- There are four primary core strengths one can have: Time, Money, Relationships, and Ambition
- Your core challenge with respect to time is valuing it and making it your ally.
- It is how you handle your money that determines how money works as a core strength for you.
- People surrounded by several healthy relationships are way happier than those who aren't, irrespective of their financial or social position.
- Ambition makes us who we are and gives us a path to move ahead in life. While being ambitious is good, being overly ambitious can harm us sometimes.
- Each core strength dictates your life in various ways.
- When you align your core to your priorities, everything will start falling in place.
- The first step toward improving a core strength is wanting to improve it—and wanting it badly.

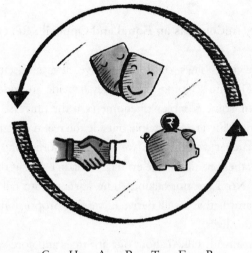

CHAPTER

4

What Do You Really Get Out of Life?

"The power of effort and the satisfaction
you get from it is underrated."

Sagar Makwana

The Three Basic Returns

"Every Action Has an Equal and Opposite Reaction."

Newton's laws of motion have always fascinated me. Despite seeming simple, they provide an understanding of some complex phenomena in the universe. The laws can be extrapolated to a principle outside the realm of pure physics as well: whatever we do in life, we always get something in return. Sometimes these results arrive even if we hadn't sought them in the first place. No, I am not talking about karma. I am talking about the basic returns that we all derive in varying proportions over the course of our lives.

Having already talked about our priorities and core strengths, I want to talk in this chapter about the returns we derive from work, relationships, volunteering, and many other areas. Although there are many kinds of returns, I will strip these down to the three bare essential categories. These are:

1. Financial returns
2. Emotional returns
3. Social returns

Financial Returns

**"I wish everyone could get rich and famous
and everything they ever dreamed of so that
they can see that that's not the answer."**

Jim Carrey

The first type of returns that we are going to discuss are financial returns. As the name suggests, this has to do primarily with the amount of money you earn in your life. It doesn't speak about how you spend or save your money.

For some people, financial returns are the sole focus of life, but can you blame them? In our imagined reality, money plays the most prominent role. We have been taught by our parents that money will help us lead the life that we want. Our parents were taught the same by their parents, who, in turn, learnt this from theirs, and so on—until this chain of conditioning perhaps stops at the very set of people who invented money.

I am not saying money is not important. It's safe to say that financial freedom must be a high priority because it helps meet our necessities such as food, clothing, shelter, education, and, of course, high speed internet. But how about asking ourselves if anything over this could be a want and not a need?

Minimalism is a concept that has grabbed my attention in recent times. It truly portrays how we have been living in a hyper-consumerist bubble that has become impossible to burst; and has made me question a lot of my choices. I am not a minimalist myself yet, but how I approach financial returns has certainly changed.

At some level, most people understand that money is just another aspect of life. Yet, financial returns are what many people subconsciously expect from their efforts. Right from childhood, we are taught that if we don't have money, we wouldn't gain respect from others, and this is exactly where we have failed as a society. There's an illusion of what our lives should look like that is difficult to break.

There was once a study that concluded that for people whose necessities were met, excess money doesn't cause a significant increase in happiness. So, if you give, say, thirty thousand rupees per month to someone who doesn't have access to necessities, it will give them an unbelievable amount of joy and comfort. They will thank you for the new lease of life. But if this same amount were given to someone who has already met all their basic needs and is comfortable enough, then it wouldn't make much of a difference in how they feel. For them, it becomes just another acquisition. Yes, they may buy something that could give them a materialistic high, but it will not last long.

This is why I believe that the need and want for financial returns is overrated in our lives. Trying to achieve financial returns alone will not help us feel fulfilled.

Emotional Returns

> **"It's good to have money and the things that money can buy, but it's good, too, to check up once in a while and make sure that you haven't lost the things that money can't buy."**

> *George Lorimer*

If financial returns are the most overrated kind, emotional returns are the most underrated. Long before we found the need to earn and trade money, human beings found the need to understand and express their emotions. It has been long proven that we developed our power to communicate with words so that we could express our emotions and share stories. Slowly these stories turned into gossip, and we haven't stopped since. We did all this for a sense of emotional fulfilment that comes from being understood by others and connected to them.

We reap high emotional returns when we feel we are in touch with our emotions and act with authenticity. We are aware of what we feel, we identify where we slip, and we pursue integrity and compassion. In return, we feel joyous, peaceful, and grounded, and are aware of our ideals and strengths.

In interpersonal situations, we reap emotional returns through strong communication and shared understanding. There is something about the feeling of being understood by another person that nothing else can replace. Through this understanding develops mutual affection and trust.

As human beings, we have a primal need for strong emotional returns. Unfortunately, we often start to replace this need with being famous, having lots of money, and so on.

Social Returns

We reap high social returns when we surround ourselves with high-quality relationships—those in which we are cherished for who we are rather than what we possess—and are able to partake in mutual acceptance and respect. Different people approach socializing in different ways. For many, socializing is about creating a certain image of themselves in others. Personally, I have nothing against people who like to flaunt what they have. But I do have a problem with how society is slowly turning narcissistic and envious due to this. Snobbery leads to a sense of misalignment with what we want and lowers our sense of fulfilment.

The older we get, the more difficult it becomes to find fulfilment—not because of more responsibilities or priorities, but because we start to expect and require more financial returns. Again, this is not because we need these returns, but because our society wants us to need them. Once we achieve these financial returns, then society wants us to go after superficial social returns. We are expected to show up at places and flaunt our status as if it is all that matters. Our high financial returns will catapult us into a social circle with people of a similar status. Then we will be asked to be a part of philanthropic efforts. If this is what you want, that's fine. But what if it isn't?

Social returns are generally difficult to build deliberately. They require being at the right place with the right people. Participating in broader noble social causes is one way to reap rich social (and emotional) returns. This, combined with the generosity to donate and create an impact by sharing your wealth, goes a long way. At the end of the day, building one's social capacity requires a lot of patience, effort, money (often), and a will to be more involved in people's lives.

All Three Returns Are Interlinked

The three kinds of returns do not exist in siloes. Each is connected to the other two. For example, human beings are social animals and we have an intrinsic need to be well liked by people. In India, especially, society forms a huge part of the everyday life and is a big factor in decision-making. Unfortunately, in systems such as these, there is pressure to gain quick social returns and this may lead to lower emotional returns.

Low social returns sometimes lead to low financial returns (such as when work goes unrecognized due to organizational dynamics at the workplace) or low emotional returns (such as when there's anxiety in being treated as an outcast).

Meanwhile, having high financial returns will allow you to enjoy some amount of emotional returns by providing the luxury to devote resources to self-care. Good social returns can always be expected from high financial returns *if* you are willing to use that money for the well-being of others.

High emotional returns will have a positive impact on your social returns as being empathetic and emotionally intelligent is the first step to being liked by people. Although it may not directly impact your financial returns, the tendency to be emotionally aware helps you in retaining a job or working with and managing the set of people around you, and this, indirectly, will lead to high financial returns in your life.

A Broad Life Trajectory of Returns

Having understood the different types of returns, the next question is when and how we understand the need for every return. Is there a general pattern to when and how these returns start to play a role in our life? Let's have a look.

Till the age of four, all we ever wanted were emotional returns—from our parents, guardians, or the primary caretakers we grew up around. We develop a strong attachment to the people who care for us. We start considering them as our best friends and want to please them. We cry so that they would nurture us, take care of us, and give us more attention. Nothing seems more important in life than to have that attention. Our brains get wired by what we experience in childhood, and slowly, this becomes our emotional wiring till adolescence.

Then, slowly, we start to interact closely with friends. They start to become an important part of our lives. Comparison sets in and we start seeking social returns, albeit in rudimentary ways. We want to be more popular, we show off our skills, and we feel bad about our imperfections whether around looks, speech, or anything else that people can gauge about ourselves. It becomes important for us to start being accepted in society.

And then, somewhere amidst all this, even as children, we start to understand why financial returns are so important. Here's how I began to value financial returns:

I was about eight or nine years old. Ours was a close-knit middle-class family. I lived with my mother, father, two siblings, grandparents, uncle, aunt, and a cousin. The young ones in the family were doted over, especially by our grandparents, and well cared for; naturally, my emotional returns were high. At the same time, we didn't have a lot of expensive things around the house. Our materialistic wants were not encouraged. As a child, seeing my friends have many games at their home, I too wished to have a lot of games to play with, but I didn't get them.

One Sunday afternoon, my friend Nikhil and I were playing at his house. Nikhil's uncle was visiting them that time. An impromptu plan was made to go to see the circus that was in town.

"Would you like to come along with us, Sagar?" Nikhil's uncle asked. Being a shy child, I didn't know what to say. I must have nodded my head slightly.

"Okay, then. The show starts at six, and we leave at five-thirty. Go ask your parents for their permission and come back here when you are ready."

Although I had been to the circus a few times with my grandfather, this was the first time I would be going to a circus with a friend, and the eight-year-old me was super excited!

I ran back home to my mother.

"Mummy! Nikhil's uncle is in town and he wants to take Nikhil and I to see the circus! Can I go? Please, please, please?" I pleaded like I had never done before.

My mom was happy to see me so excited. She agreed but told

me that I should carry some money along with me. She sent me to get dad's permission and also ask for some money.

I think the circus tickets cost around ten rupees then. I went to my dad. He had always been intimidating and I was scared. When I approached him, he was having his lunch and didn't look like he was in too much of a good mood. I still went ahead to talk to him. I was so eager to go to the circus with my friend.

"Papa?"

"Hmm?" came the reply in a stern voice.

"Papa, can I go to the circus with my friend?"

"Why are you asking me?" His face looked visibly tired and irritated.

"Well, I need . . . umm . . ."

"EXCEPT MONEY, ASK ME ANYTHING!" he roared.

I took a step back and ran to my mother, crying. I remember her trying to comfort me. She felt bad, but what could she do? She too had tears in her eyes.

It has been more than twenty years since the incident and yet I remember it vividly. Of course, I realize today that I can't give it too much power; I also understand that my father's anger may have been misdirected.

Yet, it was on that day that I realized the worth of financial returns. That day, I didn't want emotional returns from my mother. I didn't want social returns from friends. I only needed the financial returns that my father had signalled he couldn't provide. I realized that if I wanted to lead a happy life, I need good financial returns.

Of course, I was wrong. But the message was imprinted; the mould was set. It would be a long time before I realized that there is much more to life than earning money.

I am sure most of you can recall some impactful incidents that made you realize the importance of certain types of returns. We always yearn for what we don't have. That's why pampered kids yearn for love and meaning when they grow up, and many who didn't have a lot of money while growing up want to lead materialistic lives.

Just like how some people suddenly realize that financial returns are what will help them get by, there is another group of people who take financial returns for granted. This group of people probably had everything they wanted as children. They pointed at something and they got it. Slowly, they become conditioned to think that everything around them can be acquired, and nothing can stop them. This kind of thought process can be quite inhibiting. This sense of entitlement is hard to shake off.

What we need to understand is that there should always be an effort to gain returns, be it financial, emotional, or social. Taking something for granted is easy. Unfortunately, sometimes it is too late before one realizes that this is a toxic behaviour that needs to stop. This includes taking relationships and social interactions for granted, too.

The power of effort and the satisfaction you get from it is underrated.

Every return that you get depends only on you. If you think that you are not getting enough emotional or social returns, then please look for the reason. We were always designed to live with less. As human beings, we survived the harshest environments, the worst famines, and battled with the most ferocious animals. And we have, as a species, emerged successful. This is because we are geared for survival; to constantly work on what will help us protect ourselves from all the unfathomable issues that may crop up. What we were never built for is a mechanical, stilted life surrounded by goals, goals, and more goals, with an excessive focus on material gains. This quest for more and more has given us less time to think about what we need for ourselves.

Interpreting Your Current Returns

We now arrive at the most important part of the chapter. This section will help you understand what returns you already derive from life. Each of us reaps certain returns more than other returns due to our core strengths. Remember the quiz you took in chapter 3 to know your scores for the four core strengths? Note them down in the table below.

Core Area	Average Score
Priorities	
Money	
Relationships	
Ambition	

You will now map these scores on a chart and analyse them. Consider a chart with two axes as shown.

Imagine that you got the following scores in your test:

Time (Priorities): 3.80

Money: 2.20

Relationships: 2.80

Ambition: 3.00

You can mark the scores on the scale as shown below.

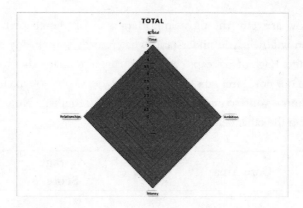

When you start mapping the scores onto this map, you need to connect them with straight lines, such as shown below:

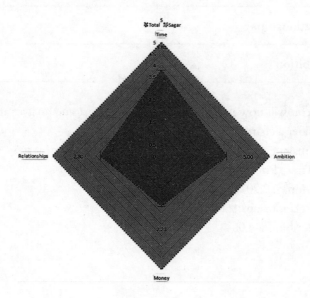

Now, it is time to combine all the scores onto a single chart:

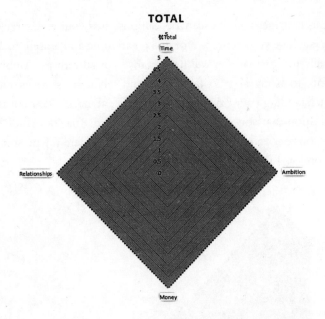

Now that you have plotted your core strengths onto the map, let us discuss how you can infer your dominant returns. The chart lets you understand what kind of returns you currently derive from your core strengths. Here's a short disclaimer: The inferences I describe next are part of a framework that I have developed over the course of mentoring, observing, and coaching people over the years. Based on different combinations of core strengths, there are different scenarios that may play out.

Scenario 1

Let us consider the first scenario. Suppose that your core strengths (areas where your score is 3 or above) are time and ambition. This usually means that you will have high financial returns. Ambition points to being able to take risks, and when risks are taken by understanding your priorities and working alongside them, it is an indication that you will receive higher rewards for your risks. You can consider an example of the graph below where the person has a score of 4 for time and 3.6 for ambition.

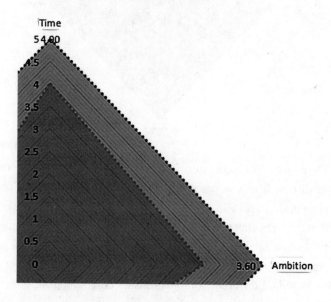

What I would like to emphasize is that giving time to your priorities and constantly working on them is important. It doesn't matter who you are or what your schedule is like. If you can manage your priorities well and focus on them in the right direction, you will end up spending time on powerful things in your life. This will naturally lead to higher financial returns.

Scenario 2

The second scenario is when one's scores on relationship and time are high. This results in high emotional returns. Imagine being the giver in a relationship and also being able to prioritize your day so well that you get your tasks accomplished. This is the story of my wife, Devangee. She is a natural giver. She takes care of everyone around her and will do anything to keep them happy. To top it all, she's good at everything she does and understands how to manage her priorities well. This helps people place a lot of faith in her and trust her with all their heart. This also results in high emotional returns for her because when people around her are happy, she is happy. In the graph below, consider that a person has scored 3.8 for time and 4 for relationships.

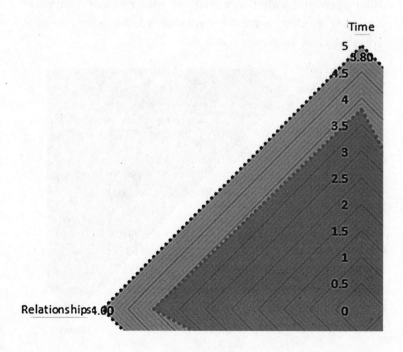

Remember, one also derives high emotional returns when they focus on cultivating an authentic connection with themselves. Someone with a high time score and whose priorities involve reflection and self-care will derive high emotional returns even if their relationship score is average (between 1.5 and 2).

Scenario 3

The third scenario is when your relationship score and money score are high. There is at least one person in every group who believes that money is just another aspect of life and loves being the giver. They are always the first to take out their wallet to pay for dinners. They are always the first to donate to a cause they feel strongly about. It doesn't matter how much they have. They will still be generous with it. The graph of such a person is shown in the example below, where they have scored 3.6 in the relationships core and 3.8 in the money core.

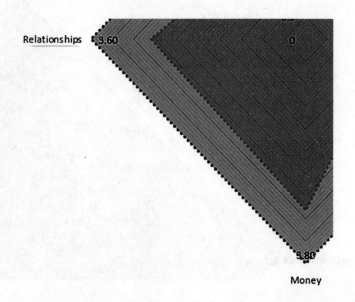

I remember a funny incident that happened in college with a friend called Nitin: One day, he was wearing a pair of trousers that he hadn't worn for a long time. When he put his hand in one of the pockets, he found a five hundred rupee note in it. This sum of money is a big deal for many college students in India, especially toward the end of the month. Nitin could have easily tucked away that note to use later for something he needed, but he didn't do that. Instead, he took a bunch of us out for lunch. He didn't think twice about it. His logic was that he didn't have the money when he began the day, and the day might as well end that way. Not to exaggerate, but back then, we felt that he was God-like to do this.

People like Nitin naturally tend to be liked by everyone around them. Ask them to lead a college political campaign on your behalf, and they will make sure you win. They tend to have high social returns, and sometimes, high emotional returns too.

Scenario 4

The fourth scenario is when one scores high on money and ambition. Such people have traits similar to those in the third scenario, except their ambition makes them shrewd and proactive about building their social circle. They tend to build a team of strong people who have high social returns, thus building an invincible fort around them. Simply said, these people go on to become strong political figures. While this may sometimes lead to low emotional returns, the power that they get through their social returns is more important to them. Politicians are sometimes assumed to be ruthless and unemotional, but this is only because they believe in prioritizing their ambitions first and relationships next. As long as a person is aware of what they expect out of their life, there's nothing wrong with valuing some priorities over others.

Consider a person who has scored 4.2 on ambition and 3.60 on money; their graph will look like this:

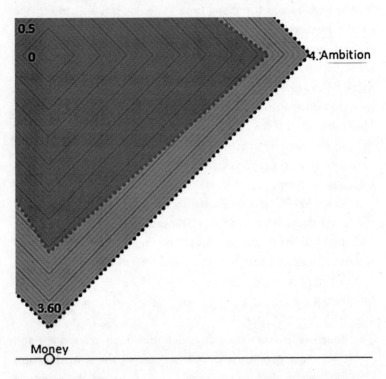

It is possible that one finds in the test that they have no core strengths at all. These people may be low in confidence and direction but nevertheless powerful in their intent. As I have often repeated, being aware is the key. Once such people understand their priorities and the returns they want in their life, it is just a matter of time before they start working on their core strengths to achieve what they want.

There are also people who score high on all the core strengths. This scenario is highly unlikely, but if it is the case, it is important that these people understand which priorities they ideally want to focus on. And, of course, there are people who score high on three core strengths. In this case, they derive two types of returns.

The main purpose of the assessment, as presented in this book, is to make one broadly aware of their strengths and areas for improvement. Although it covers the main aspects, there are a lot of other scenarios that could shape your returns; if you want to have a more personalized assessment of your chart, please feel free to get in touch with me.

What Returns Do You Ideally Need?

"The way we balance our returns is more important than the way we balance our work and life."

Which returns are the best for you? Simple—it's those that align with your priorities. It's the returns that will bring you a sense of fulfilment. Without comparing yourself to others or getting swayed by what others dictate, you need to go and seek the returns that you desire and put in the required efforts.

If your current or future priorities require you to have high financial returns, and if that, in turn, requires you to spend long hours at work, then you need to do that. Only that will give you happiness. Yes, your emotional returns may diminish, but this is what you have chosen for yourself at the moment. The people around you will either learn to live with it or decide to not be a part of your life anymore.

If you get back early from work, but immediately go out to socialize without prioritizing the relationships closest to you, it may affect your emotional returns, but then that is a sacrifice you should be willing to make if social returns are your priority at the moment. There are many who value social returns and don't care if they have enough financial returns. They derive satisfaction from knowing that they are liked by so many people, and this is important to them. Hence, the essential thing is to figure out which returns are important to you and what you want from life.

Priorities, Returns, and Core Strengths—The Three Building Blocks

The final task for us in the chapter is to check if our dominant returns support our priorities. As mentioned earlier, certain types of priorities require a higher percentage of certain types of returns. Returns themselves are a product of our core strengths, so we can then conclude that the three aspects—priorities, strengths, and returns—are interdependent. Let me explain with a simple example.

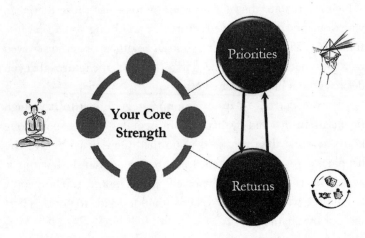

Suppose that one of your priorities is to start a capital-intensive business that will yield high financial returns. But you find that you have neither a high ambition score nor a high time score, which means that it would likely be difficult for you to gain higher financial returns. You may aspire to run a capital-intensive business, and you may even start it, but chances are that you will lose your way—unless you have someone to guide you, a person who can become your strength in the areas of your weaknesses.

This just reiterates the importance of thoroughly understanding our core strengths and our desired returns. We need to understand that to achieve our priorities, it is important that they be amply supported by the returns we derive.

A World of Paradoxes

I keep talking about the possibility of getting certain returns—with an emphasis on the word 'possibility'. Because there are certainly other factors that will determine what kind of returns we get. The beauty of life lies in the unpredictability of it, isn't it?

Let me talk about one of my friends, Karthi, to elaborate on this. Karthi is one of the most level-headed, patient, and compassionate persons I know. It is rare for him to get irked by something, and even if he does, it doesn't take long for him to calm down. In college, he wasn't too ambitious and was content with whatever he got. An average student, he would put in just about the required amount of effort to get through. He was a guy whom I felt was the most sensible amongst all of us in our gang of friends. When I think about him now, I realize that he was always bound to have a high amount of emotional returns, a meagre amount of social returns, and low financial returns.

A few years after college, Karthi was getting married and invited a few of us from college to attend the wedding.

The wedding was to happen on a Sunday morning, and the reception was planned for the previous night. The venue was a six-hour drive from my home, and my friend Balaji and I decided to travel together. Balaji is a great friend of mine, and we always end up having fun conversations.

"When are you getting married, Balaji?" I asked with a smirk, as we started our journey. I knew the question would irk him.

"I know that you are happily married, but some of us want to stay away from that happiness. Can you please not channel your inner aunty and spoil the fun of this trip?" Balaji lashed out.

Chuckling, I decided to change the topic. "Okay, okay. Let's not go there. But tell me, how well do you know this girl that Karthi is getting married to? How's he feeling about all this?"

"I was with Karthi the other day and he did get her to talk to me over the phone. She sounded nice," Balaji said, but he clearly looked uncomfortable.

"What is it, Balaji?" I asked, concerned.

"You know Karthi da. He was in a relationship with someone else earlier, and that girl broke it off with him. He met this girl soon after. I just feel that he's rushing into this a bit."

Balaji continued, "I mean, you know Karthi. He will always be the more invested one in a relationship, and I kind of feel that she is taking advantage of it."

"What do you mean?"

"This girl is pursuing her PhD. And she lives in a place that is a three-hour drive from Karthi's place. Even before they got engaged, Karthi would drive down, sometimes even on weekdays, just because she wanted to see him. Sometimes when he would go there on a weekend, she wouldn't even meet him, saying she's busy.

"I mean, isn't that a little weird? And um . . ." Balaji stopped mid-sentence.

I felt like someone fishing for gossip and didn't want to push him further. He went silent and so did I.

After a few minutes, Balaji spoke again. "The other day, Karthi was telling me that he was supporting her financially, too."

"So what? There's nothing wrong with that," I said.

"Yes, if the circumstances were different, I would agree. But with this girl, I don't know. I just feel a little weird about the whole thing."

We felt something was off. But Karthi was always this way—always giving, loving, caring, and never complaining. It has been a few years now since his marriage, which I feel is a sham. They don't live together. His wife is still pursuing some degree, and he is still working hard at some company, trying to stay afloat. They meet once in a while, but whenever they do, she is always complaining about something, and Karthi does nothing but listen. He doesn't have the courage to break off the relationship because he doesn't want to hurt his family.

Recently, I made him take the assessment of his core areas, and as expected, he got a high score in the relationship core. His time core was also dominant. This points to him getting a high amount of emotional return. But that isn't the case. Why not? People who give a lot will get a lot, but sometimes, if their destiny puts them in a place with ungrateful people, it doesn't work out that way. When contributions always seem to flow in only one direction, it starts to become overwhelming. I wish I had the courage to tell Karthi that he deserves better, but I know that he can handle himself. He's an amazing person with a golden heart, and I hope things get better for him.

In general, the greater the similarity between two people's core strengths, the higher the chances of the relationship flourishing. I often see couples who are not able to see eye to eye on the most basic things in life, and sometimes that is just heart-breaking and paradoxical.

Now let's go back to the main premise of the chapter, shall we? We all have priorities that we understand and build over time. The potential to accomplish our priorities is determined by what our core looks like. Our core strengths also determine what our returns look like. Analyzing them is important because our returns must ideally be aligned to our priorities. But this may not be the case. If that happens, then it is time to either rework on our priorities or rebuild our core strengths. The problem is most of us will almost always try to work on our core strengths to enable them to better support our priorities. But I am here to tell you that this doesn't necessarily have to be the case. Sometimes, priorities need to be reconsidered, too.

Do what makes you feel fulfilled, and not what may SEEM necessary.

The whole point of this section of the book (Chapters 2, 3, and 4) is to enable you to look within and see if you are aligning yourself to what you want to do in life. We will work on many more exercises to become more aware of the self. But for now, understand that sometimes there may be a lot of priorities that arise for you because someone else told you what is important. You may feel like you didn't even get to choose your own battles.

Similarly, your core may unfortunately be a result of how you were influenced by different people in life. You may have started out ambitious but perhaps someone in your life told you that you can't achieve much. You may have always wanted to work on your emotional self, but perhaps someone told you that that is a sign of weakness. You may not ideally want to be highly sociable but are perhaps born to influential, well-connected socialites.

Dear reader, I don't know what stops you. I don't know what bothers you. I don't know what influences you. But I do know that unless you start doing that which makes you feel like a wholesome person, you are missing the point of life. Find out what you want and take a sincere effort to work toward it. You may stumble, you may fail, you may even lose everything else along the way, but you will never lose yourself.

Chapter Summary

- There are generally three broad categories of returns we get in life: Financial, Emotional, and Social.
- Financial returns is primarily to do with the amount of money you earn in your life.
- Having a high amount of emotional returns means we have a higher level of awareness of our emotions and that we are able to connect well with people around us.
- Social returns involves having an understanding of and gelling ourselves well in the society that we live in.
- The three kinds of returns do not exist in siloes. Each is connected to the other two.
- Every return that you get depends only on you.
- Identifying your core strength and how it interplays with the returns you get is important.
- Your core strength influences your returns and your priorities interchangeably.
- At the end of the day, one should do what makes one feel fulfilled, and not what may seem necessary.

5

Attack Your Biggest Enemy!

"Be reasonable with the challenges that you wish
to solve, but be unreasonable with your efforts."

Sagar Makwana

Understanding Inertia in Your Life

Newton's first law of motion, also known as the law of inertia, states that an object at rest will stay at rest and an object in motion will stay in motion at constant velocity unless a net force acts on it.

Why are we talking physics here? I am an engineer; a production engineer (trying to pull off a James Bond vibe here). I am obsessed with physics, and I have spent a lot of time working on the shop floor of my factory, making tools, and getting my hands dirty. So, if it seems like there's a lot of physics talk in this book, now you know why. An important reason I like physics is that it never assumes anything. Everything that is stated is usually backed by airtight logic—just as with First Principles Thinking.

Now that you have understood your priorities, your core strengths, and the returns you get out of your core strengths, it is time to understand the major barriers that generally stop you from achieving what you want. As Newton says, unless a force acts on something that's stationary, it doesn't move, thanks to inertia. And right now, we will talk about what constitutes inertia in your life.

There are primarily two factors that hold you back from achieving your priorities:

1. Yourself (Yes, you read that right!)
2. Your inability to look past your circumstances, your self-defeating beliefs, and your past.

You need to understand the second factor before you can truly understand the first. So, let's begin with that.

If I could condense the solution to the second factor, it would be "let go!". There is so much that we all hold onto in life that we don't really need the world to throw hurdles at us; they are generated in abundance from within. We have all suffered in the past, and some of us continue to suffer in the present, but it is when we create for ourselves a possibility for the future that we truly start to live.

But that possibility has to be created today, in this moment, and you have to live with it every moment.

Some of you are probably thinking that this is all easy to say but difficult to do. You may say that I don't know what you are going through. And, yes, that is true. I don't know what you have been through or are going through. But I do know one thing: somewhere within you is a possibility that you are ignoring. Hear me out:

November 2020

The Diwali of November 2020 was one of the best Diwalis that my family ever celebrated. Extended family members from across the country flew down to our place in Chennai. There was a lot of drinking and dancing, and many heartfelt conversations. The dreadful first wave of COVID-19 had just about receded in the country, and people were beginning to let their guard down.

And then, it happened—towards the end of that month, on November 30, Dad tested positive for COVID-19. Soon after, Mom tested positive, too. All of us at home quarantined ourselves and consulted a doctor online. Dad was the worst affected. He had comorbidities: a high blood pressure and diabetes. We were all worried for him.

For a couple of days, we tried treating him at home, after which we moved him to a small hospital where he could receive home food and proper care. Unfortunately, a few days later, his health began to deteriorate.

On December 10, we admitted him to a multi-speciality hospital. Since the pandemic cases were slowly on the rise again by then, the hospital did not allow anyone to see him. We could only chat once a day over a video call. One night, I got a call at around 1:00 a.m. It was the doctor from the COVID ward.

"Mr. Ashok isn't cooperating much today and his oxygen levels are varying rapidly," the voice at the other end said.

"Okay," I said softly, almost unable to speak.

"If his condition doesn't improve from here, we will have to put him on ventilator support. Do you understand this, Mr. Sagar?"

"I understand. If the need arises, please do it. But do call me before you intubate him," I said, hoping that I wouldn't receive that call.

I had never been one to pray. But boy, didn't I pray that night!

It is strange how being at a point of desperation and exasperation can make one lose all positivity. Such happenings tend to shatter your faith, your strength, and your grit. It's the terror of realizing that you may soon lose a loved one; that you may soon lose yourself.

The next day, on the video call, I saw my dad with oxygen tubes in his nose. For the first time in twenty years, I told him, "I love you, Dad." He smiled, ever so faintly. "Come back soon," I whispered and with that, I ended the call.

The next morning, my dad said, "Sagar, please talk to some doctors and find out for how long this will continue. I don't like this anymore." He was not one to complain, and I could sense desperation in his voice...one that almost sounded like fear.

Do you know what causes the greatest fear in somebody? It is seeing that one person whom you consider as the strongest, that one person whom you feel can never fail, start to fear something.

A few hours later, I decided to go to the hospital and talk to the doctor to see what was happening. She asked me to sit in the waiting room. Then she met me and handed me a bottle of water.

I told her that I just wanted an update and to know when I could take my father back home.

She was silent for a while. She seemed almost too hesitant to speak. Then she spoke.

"Sir, I think we need to put Mr. Ashok on ventilator support," she said and waited.

"But . . . But . . . I thought . . . He was getting better, no?" I managed to say.

"We are doing our best, sir, but right now we don't see a way out," she continued.

There was nothing I could do there. The walls were closing in. I felt claustrophobic all of a sudden.

"Can I talk to him at least?" I asked, desperately.

"No, sir. I am sorry. We don't have the time."

"Well . . . Go on then . . ."

It was December 14, 2020; three days before my birthday. It was also the day I last heard my dad's voice.

On my birthday, I went to meet him in the hospital, wearing a PPE kit. He was unconscious, but the nurses said he could hear me talk. I touched his feet and asked him for his blessings.

"Are you listening to me, Dad?" I asked, holding back tears.

The next moment, almost as a reflex, he tried to lift his hand, just a little, as though he were trying to bless me.

That blessing was all I needed for the rest of my life.

A few more days passed, and each day produced a challenge of its own. But even as his condition deteriorated, he wasn't one to give up. He remained optimistic. My son, Aarav, was two at the time, and Dad was extremely fond of him. Maybe that's why he kept fighting—so that he could play with his grandson, hold him in his arms, and make him drink his favourite amla juice just one more time.

On December 29, 2020, sitting beside my dad, I made a video call to Aarav from my phone. While looking at the phone, I could see a tear in my dad's eye.

He lifted his hand and caressed the screen with his fingers as if he could touch Aarav. That moment will remain in my mind for as long as I live and remind me of how there's nothing more important in life than being able to love someone while they are still around.

The same day, the doctor helped my dad slowly stand up on his feet. 'HAPPY PROGRESS!' I thought to myself. The doctor told me that Dad was slowly improving, and that he will be taken off the ventilator in two days.

Well, they did remove him from the ventilator two days later, but not because he got better. But because we lost him.

Even though Dad had tested negative for COVID by then, he succumbed to secondary infections. I lost my guru, my mentor, my strength, and a part of my soul, all at the same time.

That day is what I would define as a dark day.

For a long time, I thought I wasn't allowed to say that I can't move on. I wasn't allowed to grieve his death too much. I wasn't allowed to cry. Because that is exactly what my dad would have wanted me to do.

But that's not what I did. I cried. A lot. I still do, sometimes. I told myself that I couldn't move on. I couldn't picture a life without him. I couldn't step into his work cabin for a few weeks after his death. I avoided looking at his picture on the wall. I stopped talking about his death to anyone. I was in denial.

I lived in that denial for a few weeks. I stopped taking care of myself and kept cursing my destiny for letting this happen to me. I suddenly felt lost and kept slipping into a black abyss.

Then, one day, I chanced upon my dad's diary. Something that he had written on the side of a page caught my eye. The ink had smudged a bit, but I tried hard to read the message. It said:

"The day that our reason to be in this world is over, we die. NOTHING else can call on death."

The words hit me hard. It felt like he was speaking to me from beyond. I could understand what he was saying. I realized that I could curse my destiny and cook up hundreds of stories as to why this was happening to me, but at the end of the day, I have to acknowledge that he was no more and live my life . . . until MY reason to be in this world gets over.

Right there, I decided to start looking at what best I could make out of my life and put the right foot forward.

I continued to read the diary. There was so much more written, but I would like to share just one more line.

"Yun hi Chala Chal Rahi, Yun hi Chala Chal Rahi, Jeevan Gaadi hai Samay pahiya. Aansu ki nadiyan bhi hai khushiyo ki bagiya bhi hai, Rasta Sab tera take bhaiya"

(Our life is like a car and time is like its wheels, and we just have to keep going with the flow. Sometimes, there's a river of tears on the way, but there is also a garden of happiness; and all of this awaits you.)

This is a line from a Hindi song from one of his favourite movies. The line spoke to me; it told me that I ought to be living in the present. Yes, time is never going to stop, and life will continue, but as long as I stay in the moment and live with pain or joy, without denial or escapism, I will always live a full life.

Then one day, I took a pen and paper and started to jot down all the things that I was telling myself because I didn't want to accept the reality of Dad's loss. I used a table to write the same:

Incident	How I Held Myself Back
Dad passed away	I kept cursing my destiny, silently demanding to know why this had to happen to me. I avoided responsibilities that were earlier handled by my father, thinking I didn't sign up for this. I allowed myself to get distracted from work, thinking I didn't deserve this. I kept telling myself that I should have been closer to him, and that I should have spent more time with him. I kept beating myself up for never telling him how much he meant to me.

Now, let me direct the focus back toward you—think of everything in your life that holds you back. These could be minor issues, such as the slight insults of childhood. Or they could be issues of enormous significance. Then, I want you to think of what statements keep playing in your head when you think of these incidents. So, let's go. In the table below, write down the incidents and your self-defeating beliefs about them.

Incident	How You Hold Yourself Back through Negative Affirmations or Beliefs

Changing the Narrative

After I wrote down everything that was impeding my progress, I brainstormed on how I could learn and get stronger from what happened. I tried to change the narrative so that I was no longer stuck in my old narratives.

Incident	The New Narrative
Dad passed away	When confronted with a task, instead of thinking that it could have been easily done if only Dad were there, I can focus on doing what he would do if he were present. This gives me the power to focus on solutions rather than problems. It gives me a different perspective on issues—the kind of perspective that Dad would have given me had he been there.

This doesn't mean that I have made peace with his loss, but today, I know that I need to get back to what I was doing; I need to create a possibility for my future and live in the present to pursue that possibility.

Similarly, whenever you think of the incidents you have listed above in the table, try to steer clear of the usual narratives. Instead, focus on what they have taught you, how they have empowered you, and so on, and your perspective will change. Why don't you try this immediately with this exercise and see how it makes you feel?

Incident	The New Narrative

Stripping Away Your Mental Barriers

This chapter primarily deals with three essential and transformative truths: We are not our circumstances; we are not our self-defeating beliefs; and we are not our past. The problem here is quite evident:

1. We believe that whatever happens to us is an obstacle that is difficult to overcome.
2. We keep dwelling on the belief that things won't work out for us because we don't deserve it or because we are just not capable enough.
3. We continue to live with failures and hurtful emotions from the past and assume that things won't work out because they didn't work out the last time.

You Are Not Your Circumstances

This is the most common thought pattern I see in people when they want to achieve something —thinking that they are a product of their unfavourable circumstances. There is even a term for it today: 'VICTIMITIS'. Just as I initially did in the story that began this chapter, we keep blaming the circumstances around us for being unable to achieve something. Here are some statements that I usually hear from people:

- The market is not conducive for business.
- I don't look too good. No one will like me.
- This challenge is too big for a person of my stature.
- The government's policies are just not right.
- I did begin the project, but then this big problem hit me, and now I just don't have the courage to go on.
- I took all the effort, but still, my luck is so bad that something or the other keeps going wrong.

Yes, there ARE circumstances that you can't control, and this is a difficult thing to accept. But acceptance is the first step to understanding that as an individual, your efforts will always make you resilient and powerful over your circumstances, only your mind is trying to tell you otherwise.

It was November 2012. I was working with Tata Motors, and my team was assigned to an outbound training program in Uttarakhand. It was a training program that required us to spend time on a mountainous terrain for ten days, wherein the first five days involved living in a tent and taking part in various adventure activities, and the next five days involved a rigorous trek.

The timing of the program coincided with the festival of Diwali (a time when families usually got together for festivities). Naturally, we made our displeasure clear to the HR, but they were clear that there was no changing the dates, and that we couldn't miss the training. We kept a long face and cursed our circumstances for not letting us enjoy Diwali with our families.

This trek involved covering treacherous terrain and difficult-to-navigate roads, and there definitely was some element of risk involved. We were made to sign a liability waiver that said that we couldn't hold anyone liable in case of injury or even death.

There were moments in the trek when I feared for my life. But we were surrounded by so many trainers who pushed and inspired us every time we felt demotivated. This is when I met Arunima Sinha. Arunima was one of our trainers in the program and was trekking along with us to the mountain top, much to our awe. Why? Because Arunima walked with a prosthetic leg. Every moment that we spent with her felt inspiring. One day, one of us found the courage to ask her:

"Arunima ma'am, how did you lose your leg?"

She took a moment to compose herself and then spoke:

"In my early twenties, I was a national volleyball player, and my dream was to join the paramilitary forces. One day, while travelling by train to appear for an interview for the CISF, a gang of robbers tried to steal my bag and get hold of my gold chain.

"But I resisted and wouldn't let go of my bag. The robbers then pushed me off the train. I fell off the train just while another train was passing by on the adjacent track. The train ran over my leg and crushed it below my knee.

"It took seven hours before someone could carry me to a hospital, and by the time I reached there, it was too late to save my leg. The doctors had to amputate it to save my life."

Her voice didn't quiver the slightest as she spoke this. No one uttered a word.

"Four months later, I was given a prosthetic leg and it was then that I, right there in the hospital, made a decision. I decided that I wanted to climb Mount Everest, and I am on that journey right now with Bachendri Pal ma'am," she finished.

I don't know who it was, but someone started to clap. It took a while for everyone else to join in the applause because we were in a trance. There we were, a group of fresh graduates, cursing our fate that we had to spend Diwali in training, wondering when we would go back home to meet our families. And we were sitting in front of a woman who didn't let the worst of circumstances overcome her grit and determination. No one said it, but I am sure most of us felt ashamed of ourselves.

About six months later, in May 2013, Arunima Sinha started her journey to climb Mount Everest. Her journey wasn't an easy one.

On her way to the peak, she took three hours to traverse a steep climb that would usually take an able person two minutes. The wounds on her leg had not healed yet. Even the Sherpas were afraid to accompany her, but her will to succeed was stronger than anything else. Her prosthetic leg even fell off once during the climb, and her oxygen reserves had almost depleted just as she neared the top of the mountain. Yet, the fear of death did not deter her. No one expected Arunima to get out of this alive but she wasn't going to be held down by her circumstances.

Finally, she did it and became the first female amputee to scale Everest. Her journey continues to inspire many people. What makes me feel in awe of her is that it was so easy for her to become a victim of her circumstances, and yet she didn't allow that to happen. While she was recovering from her surgery, the Indian Railways offered her a job. For someone else in her state, this would have sufficed but Arunima wasn't one to settle. She wanted to scale greater heights, literally and otherwise, and set her mind to it.

She knew that her circumstances were out of the ordinary, but she believed that she was, too.

You Are Not Your Self-Defeating Beliefs

If our mind doesn't stop us from doing something we really want to, is it even our mind? There are a lot of games that the mind plays on us, and one of them is to pin our beliefs against ourselves. These beliefs are generated due to past mistakes, issues that we encountered, but mostly they are generated from negative thoughts. What we fear doesn't turn out as bad as we predict it to. Yet, we keep thinking negatively, and a belief is formed. This belief stops us from taking steps that will propel us forward.

This usually happens to people with a low ambition score, wherein they start dwelling on their own self-defeating beliefs and declare that they can't do something. Working on yourself and making yourself think otherwise is an uphill task that only you can conquer. I love this quote by Henry Ford that sums this up:

> **"Whether you think you can, or**
> **you think you can't—you're right."**

To make you understand how one can overcome self-defeating beliefs, I am going to talk about one of my favourite sporting teams—Chennai Super Kings (CSK). The year was 2020, and since the start of the Indian Premier League in 2008, this team had always managed to be in the top four of the league table. Often, they reached the finals of the game and even won the trophy thrice, but 2020 was bound to be different. Things just didn't go right from the beginning of the tournament, and for the first time ever, they ended up being the second last team in the league.

They were ridiculed as a group of old people bunched up in a team and were promptly called "Dad's Army." Their captain, M.S. Dhoni (often referred to as MSD), who had been considered a legend thus far, had turned 39 that year, and people started to write him and his team off. So much so that during the last match of the season, one of the commentators asked him if this was the last match of his career with CSK. MSD retorted: "Definitely not!"

What he said gave supporters a shimmer of hope, but many had already lost their belief in the team. To make things worse, this was one of those years when the player line-up was meant to be shuffled considerably, but due to the pandemic, that could not happen. Hence, CSK had to continue with the same team except for one or two changes.

Gauging by the team's body language, it seemed like they too had realized a lot of work was in store if they wanted to make an impact in the 2021 season. It was clear that their confidence was lost.

Before the start of the 2021 season, critics believed that CSK was again going to falter and not going to reach the top four. Not one critic believed that they could make a comeback. It was quite possible that the fans themselves felt this way. Yet, when they came back to play on the field, things looked different.

They ended up as one of the top two teams and eventually went on to win the trophy in style. The critics had to eat their own words, and the belief that people had in CSK was back.

So, what changed in a span of six months? I feel that there are three things that changed the scenario for them:

1. They understood their mistakes from the previous season and were ready to course correct.
2. They built their team around the same core group of players, while also compensating for some known gaps in the team.
3. They vehemently continued to back the core group of players despite crowd consensus screaming otherwise.

The third point is what fascinates me the most. CSK is a team that usually doesn't change their players much, and rightly so because their team has, for the most part, proved to be a winning formula. But 2020 was different. They ended up changing their team more than they normally would; it seemed that they didn't believe in their own players. Naturally, in 2021, when one of their opening batsmen, Ruturaj Gaikwad, didn't play well in the first two matches, people expected another axe. Everyone called for it. But the coach and the captain kept backing him. In the third match, he ended up scoring worse than he did in the first two. This time, it felt like he wasn't going to be allowed to continue. There were better players in the dugout waiting for a chance.

In the fourth match, when the teams were announced, they continued to back Ruturaj. Once again, the critics were onto them, quickly announcing that CSK was not learning from its mistakes. But in the fourth match, Ruturaj lived up to the trust that the captain and the coach had in him. By the end of the tournament, he ended up being the season's highest run scorer. It was an unbelievable turnaround, and the most fun thing for me was to watch the critics take back their words yet again.

This was a team who had been there, done that so many times that people just expected them to perform. One bad season was not going to hurt their case. But even when their belief quivered ever so slightly, they continued to back their abilities and their players. They shirked the self-defeating belief that things were just not going to go right hereon, and this was the biggest reason for them to come back so strongly and become again a team that everyone envies.

You Are Not Your Past

Getting bogged down by the past is a classic case of the sunk cost fallacy. In economics and business decision-making, a sunk cost is one that has already been incurred and cannot be recovered. As individuals, we commit the sunk cost fallacy when we continue a behaviour or an endeavour for the sake of previously invested resources (time, money, or effort). For example, we sometimes order too much food and then overeat just to get our money's worth. Similarly, many of us are prone to hold on to a past relationship even if we see it going nowhere just because we feel we have already invested so much time in it. We realize that a project we have been working on is a failure in the making, but we don't let go of it because of the time and effort that has gone into it.

Sometimes, being stuck in the past hurts us so much. Despite that, we don't let go. We don't realize how much mulling over the past can affect our life. Our inability to move on from what happened months or years ago weighs us down, preventing us from living our life to the fullest. Let us now talk about a man who changed how his past weighed down on him.

Warrick Dunn was born in 1975 and was raised by a single mother who worked as a police officer in the US. He was also the eldest in a family of six children. In high school, Dunn became obsessed with playing football, and by the time he turned 18, he became one of the most sought-after athletes. He felt that it was now time for him to do his part to support his mother. Unfortunately, that dream was short-lived.

Two days after he turned 18, in 1993, his mother was killed in a bank robbery. The accused was one by the name of Kevan Brumfield. He confessed to the crime and within two years, a jury awarded him the death penalty. But as is common in many such cases, even though the verdict was granted, the sentence wasn't delivered due to a pending appeal.

Meanwhile, Warrick Dunn was devastated. His mother was his inspiration, support, and the only source of income for the family. Fortunately, his high school football coach supported Dunn to take up football as a career, and Dunn was able to support his family of five siblings through it. He became a father-like figure at an age when he was supposed to have his share of fun. His mother had always dreamt of seeing him play for the NFL, and Dunn went on to fulfil that dream in less than four years after her death. It seemed like he was fuelled by passion as well as the need to support his family.

The same year that he started playing for the NFL, Dunn also established the Homes for the Holidays (HFTH) charity program in honour of his mother. Through this foundation, he helped single mothers to start a new life for themselves without the burden of debt. He had seen his mother struggle to make ends meet while accommodating him and his siblings, and this was the main motivation behind starting this charity.

Even as he continued to build a successful career in the NFL, Dunn struggled to overcome the loss of his mother. So much so that for a long time, he was not able to develop a close relationship with anyone in the fear that he might lose them some day. Dunn has openly talked about how he had to go through years of counselling to overcome this fear. But the most defining moment of his life was when he decided to meet his mother's killer in prison in 2007, about fourteen years after the incident took place.

People couldn't believe he wanted to do this, and the days leading up to the visit were unsettling for Dunn. There were a lot of times when he questioned himself about this decision. One day he was ready for the visit and another day he wasn't. There were so many questions that he wanted to ask his mom's killer and he was fully aware that Brumfield might not say anything at all.

Finally, the day came when he met Brumfield in a small break room in the prison, surrounded by Brumfield's lawyers. After a few moments of awkward silence, Brumfield spoke first. He explained how he has changed as a person, that he shouldn't have done some of the things that he did and that he has grown into a better human being. He apologized for what happened to Dunn's family.

And then he said it.

"I didn't kill your mother. They got the wrong guy."

Dunn knew that he was lying. He had already been warned about this happening as Brumfield had an appeal pending in court. But what do you say to a guy who confesses to killing your mother only to deny it twenty years later?

Dunn decided to tell him about what that night had done to him and how it had changed his life. He told Brumfield that when one loves somebody like he had loved his mom, it is as great an emotional experience as any. He wanted Brumfield to know that while growing up as a kid, he had wanted to be a husband and a dad. He wanted him to know that what Brumfield had done that night to his mom ruined a lot of that for him.

By this time, everyone in the room had tears in their eyes, including Brumfield.

Finally, Dunn looked at Brumfield and told him:

"If you didn't do it, I don't know why you are here today, but I know why I am here today. I am here because I need to forgive somebody. I am here because it has been fourteen years and it's time for me to move on. I was searching for answers. I've been going to counselling. I've started to smile again. I've started to laugh again. I even had my first drink two years ago during a fun moment. It is time for me to forgive and move on."

Everyone went silent. He had said it. He was there to forgive.

Brumfield was silent for a moment, and then stuttered, "Why now? Why meet?" Dunn told him that he was finally strong enough to do this, and that years of counselling had made this possible. Brumfield told him not to hold onto his anger anymore, and he said that he prayed for Dunn and his family. Dunn answered that God had a path for all of us, and that he was happy that Brumfield's life hadn't been taken away. He told Brumfield that it took him a long time to stop blaming God for that night.

Sometime later, when he was asked about this choice to forgive, Dunn said that in his mind he was clear. He had just one choice: to be bitter or to be better.

For Warrick Dunn, living in the past was the biggest burden he had to carry despite being successful at what he did, despite being a role model for many, and despite being the caretaker of his whole family. Sometimes, you have everything you want in your life, but when you keep living in the past, it is difficult to have a fulfilled life. It took twenty years for Dunn to confront his mom's killer, and on the day he did, he felt a huge weight lift off his shoulders.

Most of us don't carry the burden of such a heavy, life-altering past, and yet, we don't tend to let go. Living in the past is like saying that the road is wet because it rained a few months ago. Let go of it. There is nothing left in the past.

Getting Out of the Trap

So far, we discussed three traps that stop us from moving ahead in our lives. Along with these, there's a related problem—being asked to distract ourselves from these traps. A lot of self-help gurus tend to make statements such as these:

"It is all in your mind; forget about your problems."

"If you want to achieve something, go ahead and achieve it. There is nothing else you should look at."

"Don't focus on the problems. Focus on the goals."

These methods may work but only for the short-term. You create a goal to distract yourself from your problems. Then, once you achieve the goal, you are again exposed to the problem that you ignored in the first place. No, the problem doesn't go away. Unless you accept it and realize that there are some things that you can't change, you will fall into an infinite loop of distractions.

Arunima Sinha didn't ever say that there was no problem with her leg; instead, she believed that she could achieve her dreams with a prosthetic leg. CSK didn't just go on to tell themselves that they could forget one bad season and change their team in the next one. Instead, they chose to work with what they had, and then rebuild and create amazing results. Warrick Dunn didn't just decide to ignore his mother's killer. He went on to face him, forgive him, and then move on with his life.

This idea of confronting what is important is explained by Stephen Covey in his book *The Seven Habits of Highly Effective People*, wherein he states that people who start working on themselves rather than try to control everything around them are more successful in bringing about effective changes in their lives. In simple terms, he says that we need to be proactive rather than reactive.

He explains this with a model that shows two concentric circles. The circle on the inside is the circle of influence, and the outer one is the circle of concern.

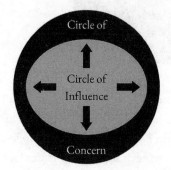

Proactive focus

This is when you work on things you can control and that expands and works on the things you can control

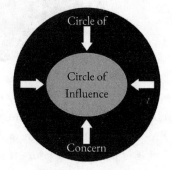

Reactive focus

When you try to focus on things that are outside your control, you let of things within your influence as well.

Covey emphasizes that people who work on their circle of influence flourish. He asks people to work proactively to bring about change.

I would like to talk to you now about a slightly modified version of Covey's model that can help you overcome the control that your circumstances, your self-defeating beliefs, and your past have on you. It is depicted below.

Circle of

Circle of

Circle of
Control

Influence

No Control

At the core is the circle of control. It is the smallest of all circles, but it is also the most powerful because it comprises all those areas that are directly under your control. This circle includes, but is not limited to, your efforts to achieve something, your work ethic, the way you build positivity for yourself, your focus on self-love, the responsibility you take for your actions, your reaction to criticism, your response to how others behave, and so on. It is a list of everything whose results depend only on you. The circle of control is the epicentre of your thoughts and beliefs, and if you learn to focus on it, nothing can stop you from building on what you want to achieve.

The circle immediately outside the circle of control is the circle of influence, and it encompasses those aspects that you don't have sole control over and can only be influenced to some degree by your thoughts, ideas, and effort. Examples include how you influence the thoughts of those around you, the image that you hold in society, and your priorities (This is not directly under your control because sometimes you have to do what others ask, such as at work.). You can also influence how your child gets nurtured, what policies they introduce at your workplace, how you get work done from your subordinates, where you choose to apply to work, and so on.

The circle of influence becomes an important part of life because what you influence can also influence you back. Therefore, whatever falls in this bucket tends to have some control over your thoughts, your work, and your beliefs. At the same time, it is important to not invest a lot of energy in this circle because you could end up investing effort in areas that don't always fetch the desired results.

The third and the outermost circle in the picture is the circle of minimal or no control. This circle includes areas that you have almost no control over. What falls in this circle is not influenced by what you do in your circle of control. Perhaps the best examples are birth and death: one certainly has no control over their place or family of birth or place and time of death. On a broader scale, the list also includes policies that the government approves (unless you are a legislator, in which case, this falls in your circle of influence), the weather, the results of a sports match featuring your favourite team, your past, your circumstances, traffic on the road, the price of most things in the market, your luck—the list is almost endless.

But there's one thing that falls in the circle of minimal control that's perhaps more significant and surprising than all the above:

results. Many people have a hard time understanding how results don't fall under their circle of control or circle of influence. Let's understand this in a simple manner. Imagine you put in your best efforts for an exam and produce your best work. If that work, however, is not what your teacher expected (Perhaps she expected a different idea or method), then she isn't going to award you marks for it. But does that mean you didn't do everything that was in your circle of control? Of course you did. But the result still didn't go your way. When my dad was in the hospital for a month, it took all my efforts, his efforts, and the doctors' efforts to keep him alive. There was not a single thing in this world that I didn't do to save his life but the result at the end was that we lost him. There was no one who I could blame for what happened. In the end, the result was not in my hands.

I have come to make peace with the realization that even my best efforts may not bring me the results I desire, while on some days, half-baked efforts fetch desired outcomes. That is both the beauty and cruelty of life.

The more time you spend on your circle of control, the more likely it is that you achieve what you want. The problem, usually, is that we keep thinking about whatever we can't control and this derails our plans. Many people constantly complain about how government policies affect their business, instead of thinking how they can ride the wave. This kind of clarity and focus is difficult to achieve, but when you do, things can quickly turn around. Again, being aware is the first step in bringing about change. To use a slightly altered version of one of my favourite quotes here:

**"Always wish that you get the strength
to accept the things you cannot change,
the courage to change the things you can,
and the wisdom to know the difference."**

The Root Cause of Your Mental Barriers

I would now like to revisit the three aspects that we talked about earlier—your past, your circumstances, and your self-defeating beliefs. If you study all these three, you will find that they stem from one source—your thoughts.

Now, relate this to the circle of control. Will you agree that our thoughts are a big part of our lives that we can control? I admit it is not the easiest thing to do, but it is certainly up to us to try.

To be able to control your thoughts, you first need to be aware of all the ways in which they manifest. Your thoughts usually fall into two clear categories—empowering thoughts and disempowering thoughts.

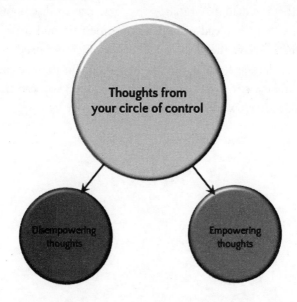

A constant flurry of thoughts is inevitable. We derive so much meaning from our world because we can think and express ourselves with emotion, passion, and logic. However, there is a case to be made about how we often let thoughts control our lives and how this changes the way we handle situations. If only we harness the power to control our thoughts, we can achieve an enormous amount of clarity. The idea is to be aware. We need to become aware of how thoughts can ruin our life and how they sometimes create ripples of negativity around us. When we can differentiate between the two kinds of thoughts and work predominantly with empowering thoughts, the meaning of life as we know it will change.

The challenge is to always be aware of disempowering thoughts and oust them from our system. Empowering thoughts emerge from battling difficulties and become the defining point of our lives—by giving us the strength, hope, and insights to go on. But difficult situations are also what give rise to disempowering thoughts that then lead to hopelessness, despair, and depression. To better perceive the glow of light, you sometimes need to enter phases of darkness, and if you use these moments to build yourself into someone stronger, one day at a time, then you can become invincible after a while.

To give you more clarity, here's a table that shows how any situation can be perceived in either an empowering or a disempowering manner.

Disempowering Thoughts	Empowering Thoughts
What if I fail?	Even if I fail, what is the worst thing that could happen?
Will society approve of this?	How can I uplift myself through this?
Will people like what I have done?	I can't change the way people perceive my activities.
This is too hard. It is just not worth the effort.	I think this is a good place to start. Let's see where it takes me.
I have never been good at things like this.	What does the learning curve for this look like?
Why is everyone better than me?	How can I be a better version of myself today?
What is the guarantee that I will get the results I desire?	The results are beyond my control.
Things never go the way I want them to.	How can I tackle this situation better?
My past is like a stone weighing me down.	My past has made me stronger.
Whatever I achieve, it just doesn't seem enough.	I am grateful for what I have.
The future looks so insecure.	Being able to live in the moment is what I would like to do.

As the Chinese philosopher Lao Tzu said,

**"Watch your thoughts, they become your words;
watch your words, they become your actions; watch
your actions, they become your habits; watch your
habits, they become your character; watch your
character, it becomes your destiny."**

Unfortunately, the other problem is that we live in a world where our thoughts are constantly shifted to suit the purpose of others. We are made to believe that we need to look and behave a certain way to be regarded as worthy human beings. It is time that we step out of this notion and shape our thoughts the way that we want to.

Let go of your limiting circumstances, let go of your disempowering thoughts, and let go of your past. Live in the moment, be what you can be, do what you can do, and the beauty that is life will start to unveil itself in front of you as a majestic force of power, inspiration, and love!

Excusitis Kills Your Dreams!

Once you remove the stumbling blocks that are your circumstances, your past, and your self-defeating beliefs, there is nothing else left but you and your effort. Once your mind has been stripped of everything that it always used as excuses to not do something, then the naked truth hits you in the gut.

But before I elaborate on this, here's an important question (one that you may have already thought of): Why am I not factoring destiny or luck into all of this? Doesn't that matter too?

Let me answer this with a quick example.

In June 2016, Venky (the smart guy among my college friends) was all set to leave for the US to do his post-graduation in Industrial

Engineering. He had already quit his job in March, and he was excited and nervous about flying to the States. All of us knew he would do well and wished the best for him.

But one fateful evening in May changed everything. While playing football with his friends at a local ground, he hurt his knee badly, and it led to a grade three ligament tear (apparently a highly painful one). The doctors suggested a surgery. But surgery or not, there was no way Venky could now start his course on time.

Venky had put in a lot of effort to get his admission in this college. He had prepared well for his exams, and he had struggled for a long time to get here. But all of that seemed to be going down the drain. It was a highly difficult point in his life. Yet, he didn't lose heart; he went on to rewrite some of his exams, did what he needed to do to join the same course in December that year. And he did.

He finished his degree on time and went on to work at one of the world's most renowned engine manufacturing companies, and I can't be prouder of what he has achieved despite that initial hiccup that almost ruined his dreams. And that, my dear friends, is what you can do when things don't work the way you want them to.

There are countless examples of men and women who went on to do unbelievable things that have changed the course of the world despite a bad card dealt to them by destiny. Deriving inspiration from them is sometimes difficult. We often think of larger-than-life examples; we feel we know the struggles of a particular famous person and he inspires us. But let me ask you a question here: Would a biography or a Wikipedia page tell you more about someone and their struggles than you seeing their struggles, day in and day out, right beside them?

So, I suggest you think of the people around you who have struggled and yet gone on to achieve what was considered near impossible. There is a case for destiny or luck, but with aspiration and immense effort, the luck factor starts to diminish in power.

Events that you cannot control will always exist. I repeat this over and over again because this thought will erupt in your mind over and over again. It is easy, after all: I have given you reasons to not blame your past, your circumstances, and your self-defeating beliefs; so your mind will start looking at what else it can blame. The answer is usually: destiny or luck.

Your destiny will make things difficult for you. If it doesn't, how will you turn out to become the person that you are meant to be? Think about all those difficult times that you faced, those desperate times that were debilitating, those moments of despair that made it seem like everything was lost. These events have made you the person that you are today. It will always be your choice to either stay disgruntled, with a "Why does it always happen to me?" attitude or believe that everything is a life lesson that makes one stronger.

Truth is that your destiny always conceives of ways to make you stronger than put you in a difficult situation. It is up to you to look at it and embrace it with open arms.

"The only person you are destined to become is the person you decide to be."

Ralph Waldo Emerson

I strongly believe that your effort changes your destiny, and that the more you evolve as a human being, the better things start to become—not because your luck gets better; rather, you get used to all the curve balls that destiny throws at you. I hope you will agree when I say that apart from everything else that works for you, your efforts will always play the biggest role in shaping your future.

Being Honest to Yourself

We are, to a substantial extent, ruled by our subconscious mind and the thoughts that it generates. The threat starts with us not being able to control these thoughts. Then slowly, this threat evolves to become a self-serving justification. It is through these justifications that we begin the drama of our lives, where we tend to let ourselves down—every single time. We become the biggest obstacle to ourselves—by preventing ourselves from moving forward. That is why I listed 'You' as the first obstacle to achieving your priorities in the beginning of the chapter. How though, you may ask, does one become a deterrent for oneself? It's quite simple: we lie to ourselves the most.

The hardest thing for anyone to do is to be truthful to themselves. We lie to others a lot (often without meaning to). But here's the thing—we lie to ourselves the most. Others will not believe our lies easily (They might not believe us even when we speak the truth, but that's for another day). Because despite all that we tell them, what they will eventually believe is heavily influenced by their perception of us. They think they know us inside out and will continue to assess us that way. It's hard to change their perception. So, fooling them is never easy. But the one person we can fool every single time, with the least effort possible, is ourselves.

Yes, it is easy for us to fool ourselves, mostly because we think we can never commit a blunder. Even when we do, we have a perfectly plausible explanation for it. These explanations and justifications go on right until we push ourselves deep into a trench of lies from which it is difficult to climb out. This illness is what I call 'EXCUSITIS.' Because the one thing (apart from an opinion) that is extremely easy to provide is an excuse.

**The truth may hurt. Most of the time,
someone else telling you the truth won't
cut it. You need to tell yourself the truth.**

The consequences of Excusitis are two-fold:
1. You continue to give reasons to not do something despite having the potential to do it.
2. You surround yourself with others' perceptions of you and believe them to be your barriers.

When you cure yourself of Excusitis, and stay true to your potential and what you believe in, you will be able to achieve a much more fulfilled life. The path to this was and is never going to be easy. But life isn't easy. It is what it is, and it is up to you to make the best of it with your efforts.

I would like to clarify an important point here. When I say you give a lot of excuses for your behaviour, I don't mean that you can achieve anything you want if you don't provide excuses. It is important that you ground yourself in the reality of your life and your core strengths. That is the sole reason we talked about priorities first and core strengths next. Because being realistic is as important as having faith in your own abilities. You need to understand and constantly assess if you are trying to be your best at whatever you do. You can't expect a ten-year-old to break Usain Bolt's 100-metre-sprint record. It is like expecting a horse to give birth to a unicorn just because it doesn't believe in anything less.

**Be reasonable with the challenges that you wish
to solve, but be unreasonable with your efforts.**

At the end of the day, unless you apply your efforts into doing what is important and work toward your priorities, you can't achieve them. When this happens, most people go back to blaming their circumstances, their past, and their self-defeating beliefs. But the actual reason is a lack of effort.

Pure effort, devoid of doubt, negativity, and disempowering beliefs is all you need. The day you stop lying to yourself, you can and will change the world as you know it. Sometimes, being held to reality and becoming aware of how things function around you brings much-needed sense of clarity to life.

Take a deep breath now. You have come so far, and you have done so well. It is now time to work on some magic that lies within you.

Chapter Summary

- There are two factors that hold you back from achieving what you want. The first one is you, yourself.
- It's not the incident but our perception of it that holds us back in life.
- When you try to change your narrative, incidents no longer hold power over you.
- You are not your circumstances, your self-defeating beliefs, or your past. They are just a part of you.
- Distraction can never be the solution to a problem. Facing it/accepting it is.
- What you do in your circle of control gives meaning to your life, always.
- How you change your disempowering thoughts to empowering ones, changes your perspective towards life.
- A bad card dealt by destiny could be just another opportunity to learn and grow.
- Most times, someone else telling you the truth won't cut it. You need to tell yourself the truth.
- You always need to be reasonable with the challenges you wish to solve but be unreasonable with your efforts.

C H A P T E R

6

Embracing the 'YOU' Within

"Finding oneself amongst all the noise and clutter
in this world is an art that one needs to master."

Sagar Makwana

LIFE is tough. It is meant to be. It is how you deal with it that defines your journey.

When I say this to people, some of them remark, "We get that life is difficult but how can we make it more memorable? Should we just bear our difficulties and move on? Is that all there is to life?" My answer is always: "Of course not!"

Below are a few lines from 'A Psalm of Life', one of my favourite poems by Henry Wadsworth Longfellow:

> *Lives of great men all remind us*
> *We can make our lives sublime,*
> *And, departing, leave behind us*
> *Footprints on the sands of time;*

Henry was writing about how great people had set examples of innovation, courage, leadership, and strength before they left this world. But today, more than ever, I believe the world also needs examples of love and acceptance. When I say love, I don't mean the love for something specific, but the love for life itself.

Do you agree that most of us carry a lot of stress in our lives every day? Sometimes, it feels like we jump from one goalpost to another without even being able to take a deep breath. These are some aspects that irk me and make me want to bring about change—change that will help people realize that there is more to life than what they see. That kind of change can start only by listening to our inner voice. By inner voice, I don't mean a voice deep within that can be heard only after hours of deep penance. I am referring to personas within us that have often had our back through the years without us even noticing this.

There are primarily three voices within all of us that we can draw upon in times of doubt—the achiever, the believer, and the comforter. What these are and how they shape our journey is what you will learn in this chapter. These three voices spring from the subconscious and collectively represent the 'You' within. This is why I often say:

The 'You' in you is talking about you. Are you listening?

I am not indulging in wordplay here to confuse you.

Each of the three You's in the above sentence represents something:

The first 'You' represents your subconscious, encompassing the three inner voices.

The second 'you' represents your current self.

The third 'you' represents your potential.

I can hence rephrase the line in the following manner:

**The subconscious forces in your current self
are asking you to take heed of your potential.**

The question remains: "Are you listening?"

Get to Know the 'You'
Who Helps You to Achieve

When I was in grade eight, I was asked to represent my school in an elocution competition organized by an elite school in the city. I had practised enough with my teachers, and I was confident of performing well. The day arrived, and I looked forward to representing my school in another institution—something I had never done before. I arrived there well ahead of time; I remember being impressed with the infrastructure of the new school and also slightly jealous.

The competition was scheduled to start at 11 a.m. We took our seats. My slot number was fifteen; there were twenty-one contestants. One after the other, the contestants went up on stage and gave their well-prepared speeches. That's when I started to feel that I was terribly underprepared. It almost seemed like the other participants were speaking a different language altogether. What grace, diction, and oratory flair they seemed to exude! A huge wave of doubt surged within, and when I went up on stage it hit me with full force. There were close to a hundred people in the audience, all waiting to hear my speech. My turn came after a girl who got a thundering round of applause that didn't stop until I stood in front of the mic.

My speech's duration was two minutes, but I concluded it in thirty seconds. And in those thirty seconds, I spoke just three words: "I am sorry."

It was a huge slap in the face for my confidence. After that incident, I felt that I wasn't worthy enough to speak on stage. Incidents such as these, especially in childhood, can leave a lasting impact. I receded into my shell and refused to participate in further competitions. My teachers too stopped me from taking part in bigger competitions; if the onstage goof up hadn't dampened my confidence enough, this further brought me down to my knees. I swore to myself that I would never go up on a stage again.

It was only years later, during college, that I eventually started to work on my public speaking skills and go up on stage. The competition there was tough too, but there was less judgment. It took a while and a lot of practice for me to get better at public speaking to a point where it felt natural.

To get from being the defeated child I was at school to where I am today feels like nothing short of an achievement. But the question I ask myself is: Who was behind this transformation? My teachers? My parents? My peers? Although these people were definitely a part of it, there was one person who continuously kept talking to me during this transformation and helped me take the right steps to cross barriers. This was the 'achiever' within me.

All of us have an achiever inside us who is talking to us. The real question is, 'ARE WE LISTENING?'

Who is the achiever within us? The achiever within us is that voice that pushes us to develop skills and capabilities that enable us to achieve something. It helps us become accountable for our time and gets us moving toward what is actionable and applicable. The achiever empowers us to take the right kind of action and effort.

There have been several situations in my life where I felt I couldn't achieve something, but eventually I overcame that fear and became better. These include being able to ride the bicycle as a kid, live independently in a hostel, organize seminars, communicate effectively with people, or even manage my own business. In all these situations, I stuttered and faltered, but eventually got better. All this while, along with experience, it took a lot of push from my inner achiever to constantly keep me working toward a better future.

Now, I want you to note down at least three instances (you can write as many as you want to) in your life where you initially felt that you weren't good enough, but eventually, with a lot of practice and support from your inner achiever, accomplished the goal. Once again, it doesn't have to be something complicated; it just has to be a situation where you put in the right effort and succeeded.

Situations in which you harnessed the inner achiever:

_____

_____

_____

Remember, the achiever in you performs two important functions:

1. It informs you what you are good at and how you can get better in areas of your strength.
2. It constantly reminds you that whatever seems difficult to conquer, or approach even, can be conquered with effort. It pushes you to invest effort in whatever seems difficult and guides you toward the right kind of effort.

Get to Know the 'You' Who Helps You Believe in You

"Mom has said that this will not work. She is really upset. Dad also isn't too happy with this. I am sorry. Please forget me. I did what I could, but I can't go against my parents' wishes. Please forgive me."

Around midnight of 11 June 2011, I received this message on my phone. It is one of the longest nights I have had to endure. I was madly in love with my then girlfriend (and wife now), Devangee. But that night, it felt like my love was crushed, broken into a thousand pieces, and thrown into the trash. Devangee, who hails from Mumbai, had told her parents about our relationship. Her parents, who had long thought that their daughter was going to marry a guy of their choice and most likely settle down in Mumbai itself, were shocked. They decided that their daughter had gone crazy, fallen into a trap, and didn't know what she was getting into. They thought it was best if she stopped all communication with me.

Being the person that she was, Devangee obliged. She dropped a long email explaining why she couldn't talk to me anymore and asked me to forget her. I cried a lot. I felt I couldn't endure the pain anymore and was engulfed by the usual darkness that surrounds a heartbroken lover; I felt I was falling into an abyss and wished that it were all a dream. But it was far from a dream—it was the gut-wrenching reality that I couldn't turn myself away from.

To make things worse, I was stepping into my final year of college and was soon to appear for placement interviews. I was also the placement representative for my class. Unfortunately, due to all that was happening, I couldn't concentrate on anything. I was selected for the final round of interviews of three major companies, only to eventually get rejected. Even my friends were surprised that I hadn't been able to crack a single interview. It was one of those phases when things were just not going my way. I started to lose sleep, my peace of mind, and even any hope of starting a career.

My friends were beginning to get worried; my mother too was in despair. All I wanted was for Devangee to be back in my life and for me to land a job. It took a while for me to realize that things weren't going to change if I continued to act this way. Yes, things weren't going my way, but it was up to me to change my circumstances. I decided to work even harder to get placed and wait patiently for my love to prove itself. It took about three months before things started to turn around.

My mother turned out to be a huge source of help during this time—she used her network to connect with Devangee's family, and they slowly got convinced that it wouldn't be too bad if Devangee married me. Slowly they came around, and things started to work in our favour. And just like that, I also landed my dream job in Tata Motors. The joining location that I was provided thrilled me—it was Mumbai! All this happened within a span of ten days, and I had to pinch myself to accept the reality of it.

It wasn't until later that I realized that one of the most important factors that made me overcome this situation was the believer within me.

All of us have an inner believer who has faith in us. The real question is, 'ARE WE LISTENING?'

Who is the believer within us? The believer is the force that enables us to channelize our grit and determination in situations of turmoil. It pushes us to believe in ourselves, reminds us of the silver lining of a situation, and makes us persist with hope until situations change for the better. The same believer that helped me weather the storm in my final year of college stood by me when I incurred losses in my business, dealt with issues in my marriage, and lost my father. There's no doubt you have gone through trying phases in your life as well—phases where it was not just your achiever capabilities but also your self-belief that helped you hold ground; where your grit and determination proved valuable. Please recall at least three such situations and write them down below:

Situations in which you harnessed the inner believer:

_____

_____

_____

This list should remind you that when things don't go your way, there are resources within yourself that you can draw on to build confidence. It is important during such times that you work on strengthening the believer in you. Because sooner than later, your achiever, along with your believer, will make things work for you.

Get to Know the 'You' Who
Helps You Find Your Way Ahead

"Once you are done with your tenth grade, you can relax."

"Things will get easier as soon as you finish school."

If you have also been a victim of such inane, mind-numbing clichés, then you are going to relate well to the story below.

Many of us have relatives who believe that life is difficult for them but easy for others. While I was studying in the ninth grade, one such relative came up to me, and as relatives always do, he began to enquire about my plans. When I said that I hadn't given it much thought, he wasn't too impressed. I didn't know what his expectations were, but I certainly wasn't too keen to live up to them. He went on to talk about his own life, struggles, and how academics are the most important aspect of life. He ended the conversation by saying, "You are too relaxed now, you need to work harder at school because once you finish your tenth grade, you will be set for life!"

The naive kid that I was, I believed him. After I completed my tenth grade, I was happy because, of course, according to my uncle, I was set for life! A few days later, I had the pleasure of meeting another relative. Much to my horror, she went on to say that tenth grade was just the initial step and that I should focus on the twelfth grade because only after that will I be set for life.

I thought, "Umm, maybe she is right . . ." and I put in a lot of effort over the next two years, finished my twelfth grade, and was absolutely elated on the day of the last exam. I was finally set for life, after all.

Then someone else came along and told me to finish college before feeling content because twelfth grade was apparently just another step. Once college is done, I will be set for life, they said. It did make sense, so then I looked forward to finishing college, but someone else came along (phew!) and told me that finishing college was just another step. The ideal thing to do would be to get a good job for myself, and then I will definitely be set for life.

I was soon getting accustomed to this game. People just kept changing the goalpost and expected me to reach there for no apparent reason. Once I got a job, I was asked to get married. Then I was told that I was not utilizing my potential in a regular day job and that I should become an entrepreneur. When I started out as an entrepreneur, I made a few losses. I was then told to work harder. Then, when I started working twelve hours a day, seven days a week, all through the year, I was told that I wasn't spending enough time with my family and that I should lead a more relaxed life!

It seemed like life had come full circle, from people thinking that I was too relaxed as a teenager to people thinking I wasn't relaxing enough as a grown up!

I was tired, not physically, but mentally. I felt I was living my life not according to my standards but by someone else's. Whether I should work for twelve hours or six, whether I should be employed or start a company—all these decisions seemed to have been pushed onto me either by other people or by situations and priorities.

Somewhere down the line, I realized that I couldn't continue to live in this manner. After giving it a lot of thought, I took a firm decision to start focusing on what I truly wanted. I decided to do things apart from work, things that I truly enjoyed—conducting training, conducting seminars, and even writing this book were a part of that transformation. This doesn't mean that I stopped working in my factory altogether. It's just that I also started to focus on areas that gave me happiness. Even at work, I started taking on responsibilities that I was comfortable with and recruited people to work on problems that I wasn't happy solving.

Whatever I did in that span of two to three years changed my outlook toward life. I started to feel fulfilled; I was able to see endless possibilities; I stopped getting angry; and I stopped blaming others for what was going wrong with my life.

Soon, I realized that all this wouldn't have been possible if I hadn't listened to the comforter within me.

All of us have an inner comforter who acts from our limbic brain. The real question is, 'ARE WE LISTENING?'

Who is the inner comforter? The comforter within us is the voice that constantly guides us toward what gives us joy and away from what doesn't. It guides us toward tasks that we will get enthused about, challenges that we will enjoy taking on, and activities that will bring us joy.

We are now going to try a quick but powerful exercise that will provide an opportunity for the comforter within to speak to us. This exercise is a powerful one, and I suggest you spend time at a quiet spot for at least ten minutes to do it. This activity requires you to exercise your imagination, and I suggest you read the next few paragraphs carefully.

To begin with, I want you to think of all those people in your life whom you love and whom you would always want near you. Now, imagine a life where you always have all these people around to support you. They are there whenever you need them. Next, imagine that you also have an unbelievably high sum of money in your account; every material thing you ever desired for is already available to you. In this hypothetical situation, you won't get poorer regardless of what you spend.

Since you have everything that you could possibly want at your disposal, you are completely at peace as far as material, emotional, and social needs are concerned. Now, here comes the important part: (Please read the following question carefully before looking for an answer.)

If such were your life—all peaceful and sufficient—as described in the exercise, where would you be headed in the next one year?

In other words, what will be the one thing that you will want to do every day for the next one year in this scenario to keep yourself engaged? Before you start to think of an answer, go through the following conditions first:

1. This purpose should be something to which you don't mind devoting at least ten hours every day for the next year.

2. You can't use your abundant wealth to skip stages or avoid effort. Even if you want to start a business or a charity, it should be done from scratch, with all the work required to possibly attract an investor.

3. You can't say that you will continue to do whatever you are doing right now. You need to choose an alternate profession, although you may not necessarily be qualified for it right now. For example, when I was doing this exercise with my sister, she said she would want to do something in psychology, although she doesn't hold a degree in psychology currently.

4. You cannot say that you will just sit and relax and do nothing; one could relax for three, five, or, perhaps, even seven weeks, but after that, they will most likely ask, 'NOW WHAT?'

5. Lastly, try thinking in terms of specific everyday activities. Please think about your daily schedule, routine, and activities, and not what you will accomplish at the end of the year. Don't say that you will run a company or a start-up. Define your position and designate it in specific terms.

Please close your eyes for a few minutes and imagine yourself in the above situation—you have the people, the money, and the freedom. What do you then see yourself do every day? Your answer should be something that deeply resonates with you. As you think about this vision, remember this:

"Stress is who you think you should be.
Relaxation is who you are."

(A Chinese Proverb)

Write down your answer below. It is possible that you may imagine yourself doing more than one thing, but I strongly recommend you restrict the list to not more than two items.

_____

_____

Aligning Your Comforter with a Purpose

Whenever I do the above-mentioned exercise with people, I have found that the vision that the comforter brings forth usually falls under one or two of four categories: compassion, motivation, curiosity, and enhancement.

The idea is that when the regular pressures of having to run behind money or keep others happy are removed, a person usually begins to gravitate toward more authentic goals that fall under one or more of these four categories.

Activities aimed at serving others fall under Compassion.

Activities aimed at building one's own skills or urging others to build on theirs fall under Motivation.

Activities aimed at exploring the world fall under Curiosity.

Activities aimed at upgrading others' lives or building something that could help future generations fall under Enhancement.

These are the priorities, I believe, that we humans have been designed for, but unfortunately, we lost our way somewhere during the rat race.

It is not that none of our current priorities fall under these categories, but the quantum is so minimal that our purpose or passion often gets blurred in the everyday chaos. Before we proceed with the chapter, I would like you to write down the categories that your answer from the earlier exercise falls under. For example, when I did the exercise, I decided that I would become a life coach or a mentor to help people rediscover themselves, which is also what I am trying to do with this book. This goal falls under Compassion and Enhancement. A friend of mine said she would like to explore different ancient architectural sites in India and write about them so that the world can learn about the beauty of ancient architecture. The categories that her vision falls under are Curiosity and Enhancement.

Now, go ahead and write down the role or vision that the earlier thought experiment yielded, and against that, note down the categories (compassion, motivation, curiosity, and enhancement) it falls under:

Vision in Life	Categories

Whatever your answer in the exercise, and whichever category it falls under, you will need the strong support of both the achiever and believer in you to realize it. Take some time now to introspect what skills and traits you need to realize your vision.

For example, to realize my vision of becoming a mentor or a coach, I need achiever traits such as the ability to communicate my thoughts effectively, the ability to market myself, and the knowledge of new communication tools and techniques from the best in the world. These are traits that I can learn and develop over time. Similarly, I need to develop believer traits such as the faith that I can connect with my audience and develop a rapport with them, the ability to overcome the fear of rejection, and also a genuine inclination to support those whom I coach.

Similarly, why don't you write down the achiever and believer traits that you either have or would like to develop so that you can bring your vision to life? Remember, achiever traits are skills that you can hone over time to easily realize your goal. Believer traits strengthen you to face challenges and overcome them despite things not going your way.

Vision in life	
Achiever traits	
Believer traits	

While we are at this exercise, you need to understand that your vision could change with time. Whatever happens to you and around you will generate thoughts that lead you to a stronger vision. Therefore, it becomes important to revisit the exercise every now and then.

Further, it's probably not practical for you to go after some of your goals right away. For example, in the case of my friend, because of her current priorities, she will not be able to immediately go on a trip to work on ancient architecture. Nevertheless, the point is she is aware of what could bring her happiness. While she is working on other things, it is important for her to strengthen her achiever and believer traits so that one day, when she is ready to work for her happiness, she has the necessary skills and mindset to do the same. I had mentioned in chapter 5 too that it is not quite possible for people to quit their job just because it doesn't give them happiness. What's important is to be aware and work toward something that will materialize in the long term.

The SAMDEV Model

We now arrive at the most important part of the chapter. We are going to connect the three dots—achiever, believer, and comforter—to see how they, in combination, affect our life. Consider a graph divided into four quadrants, as shown below. I have termed this graph as the SAMDEV model: the Self-Associative and Mental DEVelopment model. Consider the horizontal axis as representing the growth of your inner achiever and the vertical axis as representing the growth of your inner believer.

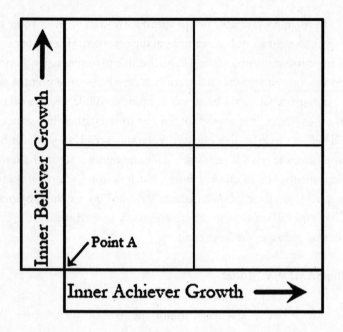

Point A at the bottom left corner of the graph is where your achiever and believer are at zero. Consider this point as the beginning of early childhood. Slowly, your achiever and your believer develop as you grow up, and you reach Quadrant 1, which is the lower left quadrant. I would like to term this quadrant as the existential quadrant. We stay in this quadrant through most of childhood, when we may not have achieved a lot or developed the fortitude or confidence that comes after facing several hardships. Simply speaking, we just exist, waiting for our time to soar.

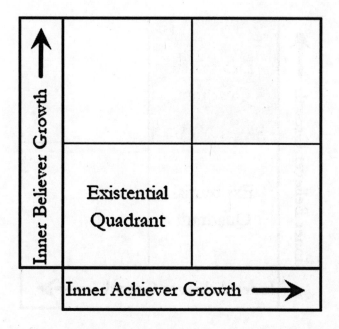

The next quadrant is the top left quadrant, which I would like to call as the delusional quadrant. This quadrant points to people who have high believer growth but low achiever growth. This is a critical quadrant because people who stay here can sometimes be delusional. They believe that they can do a lot of things, but they never make an effort to build on their skills. They live in their own bubble and hope that someone else will take them along the path of growth. Some self-styled godmen fall in this category.

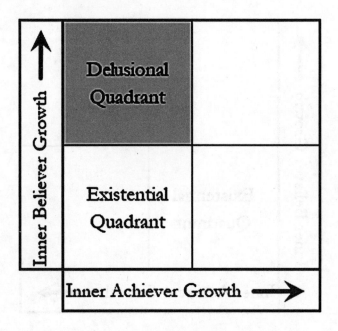

The next quadrant is the bottom right quadrant, which I call as the implementer quadrant. People who reach here have excellent implementation skills but somehow don't believe that they can do better. They learn a lot and keep pushing themselves to do work that could have rather been delegated. The problem with the people in this quadrant is that their self-esteem is usually low.

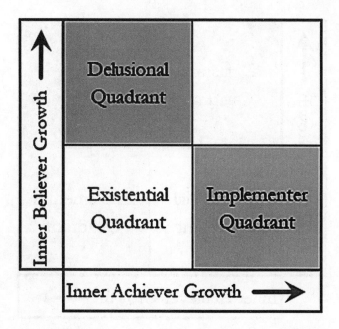

The last quadrant is my favourite, and I like to call it the phoenix quadrant. People who fall in this quadrant understand that to make something out of themselves, they need to constantly strengthen their achiever and believer cores. Even if they fail, even if they fall, they know that it's only a step toward uplifting themselves. They consider failures as stepping stones, and more importantly, understand that any success is simply another milestone on the path to fulfilling their purpose and not the end.

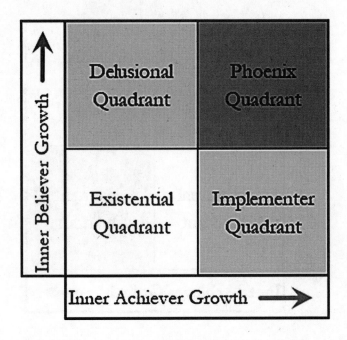

Constantly being in the phoenix quadrant is difficult, and people usually fall back into either the implementer or the delusional quadrant after a while, but there is one important factor that can change this scenario.

Changing the Game with Your Comforter

The quadrants in the SAMDEV model are defined by the role of one's achiever and believer. However, we have not discussed the role of the comforter in all this. Let us now see how the influence (or lack thereof) of the comforter changes the trajectory of our graph. Our comforter guides us toward our calling, and typically pushes us to investigate and improve our own achiever and believer traits. But what happens when we start emulating the achiever or believer qualities of someone else?

The Line of Delusion

Throughout this book, I have talked about how we have been conditioned such that we often don't even know if we are acting on our own thoughts or are stuck in someone else's ideas. This happens quite easily because as we grow from being children to teenagers, we start to believe whatever is told to us. We forget to apply our own thoughts to situations. Rather, we are not encouraged to apply them. When the believer in us merely parrots others' beliefs about us and we don't work on our achiever qualities, what happens is we move into the delusional quadrant, as shown in the next graph.

We start to believe that things will happen without us trying just because we don't see the effort others have taken. We start to lead a delusional life and create a bubble around ourselves. But sooner or later, this bubble is burst by reality, and that is when we fall back into the existential quadrant.

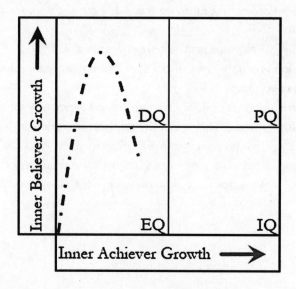

— • — Line of Delusion

Have you not seen people like this? They believe that anything is possible and that they don't need to make any effort. They believe that luck is on their side and nothing can go wrong. These people have often tasted success early in life, and they ride a high that is quite intoxicating but temporary. When they fall down though, they fall hard, and then they experience an existential crisis.

The Low Self-Esteem Line

The other scenario that is possible, as shown in the next graph, is where we take a lot of effort to work on our achiever skills, but only to the extent that others have defined achievement for us. We don't believe in ourselves enough to do much better and grow. Further, before we can push ourselves to grow, we are often put down by society:

"You can't do this."

"Boys are not meant to do this. Girls can't achieve something like this."

"Stay within your limits or else you will fail."

"Don't try to be over-smart. I have seen many people like you. They fail eventually."

Such statements slowly start to poison a person's mind, and they stop growing. They reach the implementer quadrant and get stuck there because they stop believing in themselves and stop believing in the power of effort. Then they start to reduce their efforts, thinking that there is no point in putting in more effort.

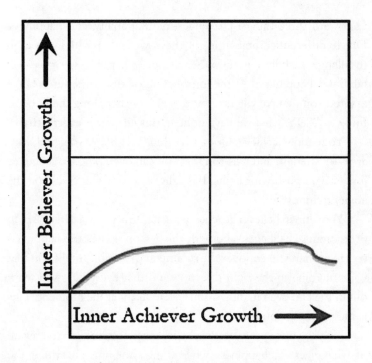

——— The Low Self-Esteem Line

Both examples show us one thing: when we start to lead our life according to someone else's wishes, we tend to fail. If we don't couple our learning with our own life experience, we will restrict ourselves. In other words, if we do not listen to the comforter within us, we will go astray eventually. This is what we spoke about in chapter 2 about not following others' maps as a reference for our life.

The Comforter Line

Let me now refresh your memory on certain concepts we learned in Chapter 2. In chapter 2, we saw that our inner compass pushes us toward three things: challenges, natural ability, and happiness. Due to different combinations of these, we end up with innovation (challenge + ability), intuition (challenge + happiness), or passion (ability + happiness). At the intersection of these lies our WHY. I assured you that we will take more steps further along the book to find our WHY; what we have done in this chapter is exactly that.

Your inner achiever does two things: it helps you find your areas of strength and tells you that you can overcome challenges as long as you push your limits. Basically, your achiever gives you the ability to innovate.

Your inner believer teaches you that grit plays a huge part in overcoming challenges, and with this lesson comes the happiness you feel when you conquer the mountain of doubt. It tells you that you are going in the right direction and that everything will work out in the end even if things don't seem like it at the moment. This is the power of intuition.

Finally, your comforter works its magic by making you aware of what gives you happiness, while at the same time unearthing the natural abilities or talent that you have to go toward it. As you follow the path that your comforter shows you, you find your passion.

When you start to work with these three aspects of your personality, you will shed your inhibitions and start living life for the purpose you were built for and not what you have been trained for. When you truly combine the power of your achiever (innovation), believer (intuition), and comforter (passion), you can achieve your 'Why.' And you will reach the phoenix quadrant.

The path that each person takes to the phoenix quadrant may be different (as depicted in the next graph). Even though the path will lead each of us to a different set of places and ideas, our job is to embrace these and settle for nothing less than reaching the phoenix quadrant.

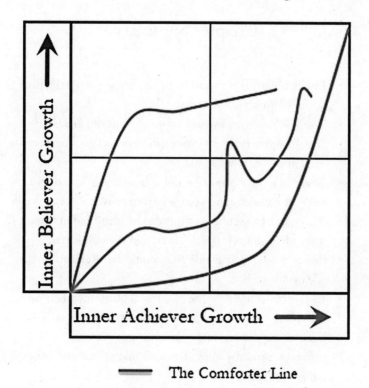

The Comforter Line

I hope that this chapter (and this book) acts as a catalyst to enable you to reach the phoenix quadrant sooner rather than later.

Finding oneself amongst all the noise and clutter in this world is an art that one needs to master.

Some people, rather philosophically, insist that we are born alone into this world and that we will die alone. I agree. But I also believe that as long as we exist, we need to nurture that one huge strength that will shape us along the way: our relationships. And in the next chapter, we are going to talk about how relationships can make or break our journey.

Chapter Summary

- Life is tough. It is meant to be. It is how you deal with it that defines your journey.
- The subconscious forces in your current self are asking you to take heed of your potential. The question remains: "Are you listening?"
- There is always a part of the subconscious mind that helps you understand your achievements.
- This part of the subconscious can be identified in three ways: the achiever, the believer, and the comforter.
- Stress is who you think you should be. Relaxation is who you are.
- Everyone starts from the existential quadrant when we are trying to learn and grow in our lives.
- When one has a high believer growth and a less achiever growth, they tend to move towards the delusional quadrant.
- When one has a high achiever growth but are not able to believe in themselves, they turn into implementers.
- Only when your achiever and believer growth happens in tandem, can you reach the phoenix quadrant which can help you face issues with confidence and logic.
- As long as you stick to your strengths, you will always be able to redeem yourself from difficult situations in life.
- Finding oneself amongst all the noise and clutter in this world is an art that one needs to master.

CHAPTER

7

Your Tribe Determines Your Vibe!

**"You are the average of the five
people you most interact with."**

Anonymous

Believe Those Who
Believe in the Idea of YOU!

**"You are the average of the five
people you most interact with."**

A lot of people say this and I see why. Many factors impact the way we think and act; one of the more significant factors among these that our future self will always significantly depend on is who we surround ourselves with. Although we mostly base our decisions on our needs and wants, the people who influence us have a much higher impact than we believe.

Think about all those times when you felt like watching a TV series or a movie just because everyone else around you was watching it.

Think about those times when you bought the latest gadgets just because you saw your friend buy them.

Think about those times when you were pressured by peers into trying something undesirable.

Think about how you plunged into the field of engineering or medicine just because your friends were doing the same.

Think about how you compared your life with someone else's based on what they posted on social media.

In this chapter, we talk about some important kinds of relationships and the impact they hold over our journey.

Over the years, we meet several people who touch our lives in myriad ways. I will credit many people for making me the person I am today. While my school friends taught me the meaning of true friendship and loyalty, my college friends taught me to be gritty and work harmoniously in a team. My stint at Tata Motors gave me the reality check I needed; I understood that many people will look for what benefits them rather than what is right. Being an entrepreneur then brought me down to my knees, and a few years of the experience gave me the strength to bear anything.

Among other things, when I was 24, I joined an association called the Young Entrepreneur School, and it tremendously shaped my professional and personal life. It changed the way I thought and gave me a lot of insight. Through this group, I also had the privilege of meeting someone who would become a mentor for life—Raja Krishnamoorthy.

When I was 26, I got my first speaking opportunity in a college in Chennai. It helped me understand my potential as a speaker. This paved the way to a few more stints, and at 29, I joined IATD to earn my Master's Diploma in Training and Development, and that turned out to be a pivotal decision that led me to understanding what I was capable of. Dr. Rajan, who was leading this company, became another source of inspiration and a great mentor.

All through ages 24 to 31, I was directly mentored by another person who has immensely shaped my life and will continue to do so: my father. I realize that I have even started to resemble him and speak the way he used to, or so people remind me time and again. Here's a story about one life-defining incident with my father.

"Sagar, who are you talking to?"

I was shocked to see my dad standing in my room. I quickly hid the phone under my pillow.

The year was 2010. I was only 20 at the time and had come back from Coimbatore for my study holidays. I was about to go back to my hostel the next day as my final exams were to start in a few days. It was eleven at night, and I was about to drift off to sleep, when I got a message from one of my close friends, Faz. She was going through some problem and wanted me to help her. What I didn't expect was my dad to have been listening.

He asked me again, "Who were you talking to over the phone, Sagar?"

I gave him my phone. I told him that I wasn't talking to anyone. He checked the call log and saw that no calls had been made or received in the last four hours. This was the phone he had given me. It had a postpaid SIM. In those days, having a postpaid connection was a privilege. Not for me though—my call log was available to my father every month. It was a nightmare!

He looked at the phone again and then looked at me. "I am sure you were talking to someone. Would you like to own up?"

He gave me that look—that look which said that if I didn't tell him the truth immediately, this wasn't going to go well.

I slowly took out a second phone out from underneath my pillow.

"Whose phone is this?" he asked. I told him it was mine. I had a girlfriend then who didn't live in the same city, and a long-distance relationship was never going to work without a phone, certainly not with a postpaid SIM! For this reason, I used a spare phone with a prepaid SIM that I paid for with my pocket money.

It may not seem like a big deal now, but we are talking about India before the Reliance Jio revolution! We were charged, substantially by a college student's standards, for every minute of a call. We didn't have WhatsApp; even Internet connectivity on the phone was uncommon in those days. The phones didn't have a touch screen, and we had to press bulky buttons to operate them. I was probably the only person in my college to be carrying two phones with him. This was probably why people would look at me and jestingly remark in Tamil, "*Periya Aalu*" (*bade log* in Hindi, meaning 'rich folks').

As my father stood staring at the second phone, I cursed myself for having two phones. How was I going to explain this to him? I was sure he was going to go through my call logs again. Intrusion of privacy, you say. Well, at that moment, I would have been more than elated to just not have my phone taken away from me.

He took the phone and started going through the recently dialled numbers.

"Who is this Faz?" he asked.

I told him that she was just a friend. He stared at me again. I swore that she was just a friend and that he could call her and ask if he wanted to, immediately regretting having said it. "Shit! What did I just do!" I thought.

He dialled her number. Faz picked up the phone and quickly realized from the voice that it wasn't me and that it could be my father. Taken aback and scared, especially given the reputation my father had among my friends, she cut the call.

"Why wouldn't she talk to me?" my dad asked.

"How would I know?" I shot back, almost in tears now. If there was one person in the whole world I was scared of, it was my dad.

He took away both my phones and walked back toward to his bedroom. I couldn't understand what was happening. My mother was standing right behind him. It was her turn now to interrogate me.

"Who is she? Do you have a girlfriend?" she asked, looking me in the eye. There's something in a mother's stare that makes you *not* want to lie to her.

I stuttered. She raised her voice a little further. "SAGAR!"

"Faz is not my girlfriend!" I muttered under my breath.

"I trust you, Sagar. You know that."

I was glad I didn't lie to her. More importantly, I was so glad that I was talking to Faz and *not* my girlfriend!

"What's Dad going to do? I don't want to lose my phone. I bought it with my own savings, maa." I looked at my mom with desperation, hoping for a positive answer.

"You know your dad. Even I can't predict his moves." Saying this, my mom went back to her room. I didn't dare follow her. I was safest in my room. Less than five minutes had passed, and my dad called for me. I was gathering my arguments.

"I haven't done anything wrong."

"She's just a friend."

"At least I am not an alcohol addict."

"I am 20, and I am old enough to know what's right and what's wrong."

"It's my life now. Don't try to butt in."

All these arguments looked strong to me. Whatever he would say, I decided I wasn't going to back down. Not today.

"SAGAR!" my dad's loud, booming voice came from his room. Unfortunately for me, my sisters had already slept, so I didn't even have their support on my side. Slowly I entered his room, fearing the worst. He asked me to sit. I looked at him, expecting him to shout at me and take my phones away for good as punishment. If there was one thing I was sure of, it was that he would never raise his hand.

But up came the hand . . . not to hit me though. He opened the drawer next to him and took out a piece of paper and handed it over to me. I opened it; in it, these words were written:

"The woods are lovely, dark and deep,
But I have promises to keep,
And miles to go before I sleep
And miles to go before I sleep."

He then looked me in the eye and asked, "Have you ever read these lines before?" I nodded. I couldn't remember the poet, but I did remember reading these lines in school.

By now, I was quite taken aback—first, by what he had just done, and second, to see that he was familiar with these lines. It wasn't that he wasn't comfortable with reading English, but I knew he didn't have formal education and was unlikely to take interest in English poems.

He continued, "I happened to chance upon these lines when I was about your age. At that point, I didn't even know how to read these lines properly or understand their depth.

"Later in life, at a decisive moment, I had to choose between a life of distractions with gambling, womanizing, and deceit, and a life of virtuousness, effort, and powerful intent. At that crossroads, this poem helped me make the right choice and the result is here for you to see.

"My dear son, I sincerely hope that you can learn this lesson much sooner than I did, and that you understand how just four lines of a poem can redefine your journey in life."

Having said that, he handed me back my phones and asked me to leave. I left, but not before turning back to see him staring pensively at me.

I went back to my bed, trying to contemplate what had just happened. On that day, a part of me transformed forever, thanks to these four lines. There I was, trying to bring up arguments that it was well within my right to do what I wanted to do in my free time—almost like a rebel. The plot twist was that my father felt the same. He realized that I had done nothing terribly wrong and that I was just trying to enjoy my adolescent years.

However, what I had never realized up until that point was: sometimes, responsibility is not about an action being right or wrong, but about where we invest our efforts. Distractions often seem delightful. They come aplenty, and then you lose your focus. And not all distractions are minor intrusions such as television, video games, or even gossip. Sometimes, distractions are activities that slowly lead you away from fulfilling your purpose in life and working toward a greater good.

This is certainly not to say that we shouldn't fall prey to any distraction ever. However, we must be able to control our urge to do something rather than let the urge control us. There couldn't have been a better way for my dad to explain this to me. If he had used physical force or anger to drive home this point, it may not have resonated so well. On that day, thanks to him, I realized this:

Love is not always about getting pampered.
Sometimes, it's about being shown the right way.

Love is also that which shields and protects us in times of despair. Although I have so far talked about my father, this statement extends to any parent, guardian, or other people one grows up around. Their love and guidance profoundly shapes our life and leaves a mark forever. As children, we get perturbed and influenced by the smallest things around us because that is how pliable our minds are. When we become teenagers, we start to challenge the beliefs we formed as children. We may even start having the terrifying feeling that we are on our own or that we don't belong to this world. This is more likely to happen when our ways divulge from those of the general community.

During all of this, how the people around us frame the narrative goes a long way in determining our progress. If handled the right way, wherein we are made to understand that any decision could impact us in a positive or negative manner, then it nurtures responsibility, ideas, and insight. However, if, for every decision we take, there is always ridicule or contempt, then we retreat into an unhealthy mindset that is difficult to get out of until much later.

The point of this message is twofold: first, if for some reason, you weren't guided in the right manner as a teenager or the people who influenced you didn't provide the right encouragement, then please reevaluate all those moments, understand that these people didn't know any better, and forgive them. Try to think about how you can let go of such memories and not let them cast a shadow as you move on to bigger things. If required, consider letting go of such toxic relationships.

Second, if you are someone who has the power to influence young people—your children, nephews, nieces, students, or even your young neighbours—then try your best to give them a clear perspective on life. Let them understand that life isn't as complicated as they imagine it to be. Let them understand that even when the whole world acts with pomp and show, they can remain true to themselves; that they don't have to submit themselves to all the notions that society sets for them. Simply put, if you had a rough time as a teenager, then do all you can to prevent the young ones in your life from going through the same.

We discussed until now how our parents or guardians can impact our lives. But in today's times, I have come to understand that this applies equally to a completely different set of people who heavily influence our years of upbringing and growth: friends.

The Bonds of Friendship that Make or Break Us

> **"Friendship isn't one big thing.**
> **It is a million little things."**
>
> *Paulo Coelho*

There are not enough things I can say about why friends are so important.

Your close friends usually mirror the pattern of your own thoughts, especially if they have been a considerable part of your life for five years or longer. Your friends can be your biggest supporters. Your friends carry secrets that you sometimes can't share even with your partners. Friends provide solace during tough times, know you for who you are, and believe in you when most people don't.

The most distinct mark of a beautiful friendship is that it can blossom for the most interesting reasons and can't be ruffled by time or distance. I believe that the most important lessons of life come not from saints, but from the best of friends, for the simple reason that true friendship is uninhibited, fearless, loving, caring, and interesting, all at the same time.

Friendship should therefore be treated with as much care as familial relationships, sometimes even more.

I have been blessed with a wonderful set of friends: cousins who have turned into friends for life, friends from school, friends from college, friends from my time at Tata Motors, friends from my journey as an entrepreneur, and even some friends from my journey as a husband and father.

Not everyone of them has seen every side of me. Some of them have seen me at my best, some of them have seen me at my worst, and some, both. This, of course, means that they each may have a different opinion of who I am. Nevertheless, they have all had a role to play in making me who I am today.

Because friends know so much about us and are extremely influential, friendship also sometimes comes with a cost: friends can, due to misunderstanding or thoughtless behaviour, derail us from our ideal path with their strong opinions or misled ideas.

When I started off my journey in training, there were a few friends who couldn't understand what I was doing. To them, running a business was all there was to life. They felt I was crazy to not focus on my business and do something new. I respected their opinion, but soon I decided to stay away from that negativity. This doesn't mean I stopped meeting them. It just means that I stopped talking to them about my training journey.

There will always be some people in your life who will not be their most encouraging selves when you go out of your way to achieve something for yourself. Please don't blame them. Either they don't know any better or they are just jealous. And people who are jealous are just people in pain. Empathize with them. Try to understand their perspective and let them be. As you proceed in your journey and start to achieve, they will be the ones who will come back and take credit for being on your side.

Yes, friends determine how you build your life. But in that process, if someone stops you from growing, perhaps you can stay away from them. After all, your friends come under the bracket of your circle of influence, i.e., you can't completely control if someone chooses to be friends with you. Similarly, you can't control if your friends support you on a path of growth. Sometimes, rather than being there for you, they may have trouble appreciating your growth or refrain from supporting you as you move forward. These are toxic relationships that you may, unfortunately, have to let go. Your life is your journey alone, and however painful it may sound, you may have to sometimes go at it alone.

The converse will also be true. At times, you may be going down the wrong path, and a set of friends will pull you out of it. You may not even realize that you are doing something self-destructive, and it is up to you to listen to your friends during such times. You must introspect and understand if the problem is with you and change your ways accordingly.

Partnership: The Bittersweet Candy

**"Being deeply loved by someone gives you strength,
while loving someone deeply gives you courage."**

Lao Tzu

So far, we spoke of parents and friends. It is natural to presume that we will next discuss the role of a spouse or partner. However, that won't be the case. Instead, we will look at another special relationship: there's often a special kind of relationship (that may or may not include your spouse) we hold with one or two people in our lives that holds tremendous meaning, value, respect, and understanding. These are people whom you can always look up to for support, advice, inspiration, and honest feedback. You may not speak to them every day, but when you do, it's an enriching conversation.

These are people without whom you can't imagine life. Even if you do lose them someday due to some differences, distance, or death, it would feel like a part of you went missing. These people believe in our priorities and purpose. Such relationships are important to cherish because as we move ahead in life and take on struggles that are far greater than us, these relationships become a tremendous source of strength. Having that one person by our side is all that we may need, not because we would be lost without them, but because with them, we feel that anything and everything is possible.

We are all going to falter and go through difficult times. Sometimes, we just need a push, a push that will get us over the edge and let us fly. And this push will always come from the relationship we hold closest to our heart, with the one who knows us inside out and understands our dreams.

Like I said, as much as one could hold such a relationship with one's spouse, it needn't always be the spouse. It could be a teacher, colleague, business partner, or even your boss. Yes, marriage does create a sacred bond and make two people feel like they are made for each other, but marriage isn't the only path to finding this person.

So, what should you do when you find one such strong pillar of support? I believe that you should spend as much time as you can with this person, because one day you will grow old and you will look around for people you can trust your life with. You will look around for people who can make you feel like YOU. You will look around for that one strand of support that makes you look forward to the next day. When you look for all these things, only that one strongly impactful, love-filled, respect-oriented relationship will give you the solace you crave for.

For me, it so fortunately happens that I found that person in my wife, Devangee. My life with her has been a bundle of moments that have made it worth all the pain, anxiety, and troubles that life has thrown at me. Even after twelve years of friendship and love, she keeps me grounded, providing me the reality checks that I need. She has helped me connect to my feelings and guided me in managing relationships that I otherwise would have ruined. She believes in me more than I have ever believed in myself and has taught me to respect women, build healthy connections, and accept others' flaws.

As is true in my case, one's spouse or partner can be an important influence on one's journey. I have always believed that intimate relationships shouldn't be based on love but on kindness and respect and giving back. Because (and brace yourself for this)—love will fade. It is bound to. Individuals change, their needs change, and their points of view change. Unfortunately, love usually blooms under the assumption that nothing will change. Lovers don't become lovers until they start getting comfortable with each other, and until their needs and points of view match. When people divulge from these commonalities, it could create a space between them that is devoid of love. And what ideally remains is the respect they have for each other. Friedrich Nietzsche said: "It is not a lack of love, but a lack of friendship that makes unhappy marriages." I believe in a slightly modified version of the same quote:

It is not a lack of love, but a lack of
RESPECT that makes unhappy marriages.

If, instead of love, partners get together because they respect each other, then nothing can pull them apart. They will bicker, fight, and oppose each other at every step, but when one of them goes through a tough time, the other will push for clarity, and provide the necessary help and support in every way possible. Therefore, I believe that the most important thing in relationships is respect.

I don't mean to say that a relationship bundled with respect will last forever. When love dies, but respect stays, the couple may break up, but not in a childish way, wherein they stop talking to each other or just can't tolerate the existence of the other. The break-up will be filled with a lot of respect, and that respect will ensure they support each other through their next phase of life. I believe that when a relationship breaks after at least ten years of togetherness, it doesn't break completely. A part of the person continues to stay with the other. And nothing gives me more happiness than to see people support each other even after proceeding in different directions. Love may be lost, but respect isn't. And this is one of the biggest levels of maturity that one can reach.

Now that we have learned about the important relationships that shape us, I want you to write down the names of people who currently hold the power to influence you. Think if these people understand your priorities and are aligned with the path that you are on. If they are, then be grateful and thank them today if you can. And if they are not, then evaluate your options. Maybe you can spend time with some others who will inspire you. Spend time with those people whose ideas and thoughts are aligned to your dreams and priorities. I am not saying it is not good to have fun occasionally or create crazy memories that will last for a lifetime, but there is always something more out there awaiting you. List the five people in your life who have the power to influence you the most:

1. _____
2. _____
3. _____
4. _____
5. _____

The Bipolar Conundrum

Relationships are work. Even the simplest bond can become a breeding ground for resentment and misunderstanding if we do not understand some basic aspects of human personality.

Like we saw in Chapter 3, different people have different core strengths. It is up to us to identity these and work alongside them. In marriage, too, you choose a person with a core that defines them. Like we discussed in Chapter 4, when your core aligns with that of your partner, the relationship becomes stronger and filled with magic. That said, there is no one person who will be the best solution for you in every situation, and you have to accept this. This reminds me of some lines that I once read in a business magazine.

"If you want a service that is great and fast, it is not going to be cheap.

"If you want a service that is cheap and great, it is not going to be fast.

"If you want a service that is cheap and fast, don't expect it to be too great."

In my family, my brother-in-law and I have a reputation for being too practical, much to the annoyance of my wife and my sister. They hate that we can be blunt about things, not bothering too much about what the other person may feel.

However, when my sister and wife want any support with getting things done or want to outsource the planning of a vacation, they don't seem to have a problem with us being practical. What seems a pain at times also works for them in some ways.

Similarly, my wife disliking socializing too much sometimes gets to me when I want to go out with people and she doesn't. However, because her social circle is so small, she dedicates a lot of time and effort to keeping these people happy, myself included. And I certainly can't complain about that.

This is what I like to call as the bipolar conundrum in relationships—expecting different things from a person as per one's convenience. The reason why you love someone could also be the reason you get annoyed with them.

At the end of the day, when it comes to people, it is just about managing expectations and understanding that not all solutions will come from one person.

When you want a solution, you go to one person, and when you want to have fun, you go to another. When you want guidance with your career, you go to one person, and when you want relationship advice, you go to another. When you want to make Goa plans, you go to one, and when you want your Goa plans ruined, you go to another. Understanding this can help set expectations right.

Agreeing to Disagree

There is another extremely effective method that has always helped me move past difficult times in relationships: agreeing to disagree.

Agree to disagree. This motto will completely change the quality of your relationships. Agreeing to disagree simply means knowing that someone else's opinion can be different from yours and that's okay.

When you agree to disagree, it doesn't mean you give in; it just means that you have the maturity to accept but not necessarily agree to another person's opinion.

Of course, this is easier said than done because our ego wouldn't let us accept another person's point of view so easily. We tend to believe that we are right based on the assumptions we already hold. In psychology, this is explained by a theory called "anchoring". An 'anchor' is a reference point of information, usually the first piece of information we receive on a topic. All subsequent decisions are knowingly or unknowingly anchored to this point.

We tend to defend our assumptions and believe that we are always right until someone shatters the glass. All these "I am always right" thoughts are usually derived from our ego. But let me tell you this: having an ego is not always a bad thing. Yes! An ego that is larger than life is terrible, but within healthy limits, it lets you stand up for yourself and your ideas and not be a pushover. In the latter case, sometimes, instead of saying, "I AM RIGHT!" we can try and say, "You may be right, my friend, but just for today, let's agree to disagree."

Volumes and volumes of books can be written about relationships, but the goal of this chapter is not to present itself as the bible of relationship advice. Rather, it is to bring about 'relationship awareness'—to cultivate a certain level of sensitivity toward understanding how relationships can strengthen or weaken our journey, and how best we can be prepared. People who have the power to influence you should understand your priorities and be able to push you toward achieving them. And when you do find someone who pushes you to be your best, hold on to them, never let them go, and learn to accept them as they are.

In the next chapter, we will talk about how to make time work in your favour so that you can build on your priorities better.

Chapter Summary

- You are the average of the five people you most interact with.
- Love is not always about getting pampered. Sometimes it's about being shown the right way.
- Your close friends usually mirror the pattern of your own thoughts, especially if they have been a part of your life for five years or longer.
- These are people without whom you can't imagine life. These are usually people who believe in your priority and purpose.
- It is not a lack of love, but a lack of RESPECT that makes unhappy marriages.
- Sometimes in a relationship it's important to agree to disagree. That is a sign of a healthy relationship.

8

Time Management Is a Farce!

"How you manage your priorities and
align them with the returns you desire will
determine the course of your life."

Sagar Makwana

This, Here, Now!

All of us wish for different things in life. We invest time and effort and eventually attain at least some of these things. However, by the time we learn to cherish what we got, we have already moved on to the next target, the next best thing. The moment gets lost even before we catch a glimpse of it. This is because we have always been told to not just set goals but to keep changing these goals forever. First, it's education, then career, and then money, family, friends, health, and if somewhere between all this we get the time, then a few moments of happiness.

Have you ever taken a step back to ask if this is what you want? Have you ever wondered what could have been if you had played a few cards differently?

"I wish there was a way to know you are in the good old days before you've actually left them."

The Nard Dog (Ed Helms), The Office

The moment I heard this line in one of my favourite shows, *The Office*, I knew that I was going to use it somewhere someday. That's how strongly I could relate to it.

When I was a child, I used to complain about not being allowed to do many things that adults did. Now that I have grown up, I wish I can go back to my childhood days.

When I was a child, I used to fight with my siblings over a bowl of Maggi. Now that I can afford a lavish spread, I just wish I can eat with the entire family seated on the same table.

When I was a teenager, I wanted a lot of money to spend. Now that I have the liberty to spend money the way I want to, I just wish for one night's worth of good sleep.

When I was an adolescent, I wanted to lead an independent life. But when I started living in a hostel, I just wished to lie down on my mom's lap one more time.

When I turned eighteen, I wanted freedom from my dad questioning all my decisions. But when I lost him, I just wished to have his guiding hand over my head one last time.

All along, I failed to understand that my goals will keep changing; that the imaginative, materialistic demands of my mind will continue to consume my time. I wish I had understood much earlier that some precious, rare moments that are often overlooked in the pursuit of goals will never, ever come back.

I want to include here two lines from one of my favourite songs, *Aaj Jaane Ki Zidd Na Karo*, written by Fayyaz Hashmi.

> **"Waqt ki kaid mein, Zindagi hai magar.**
> **Chand gadhiya yahi hai jo azaad hai."**

(Our life is bound by the shackles of time. Yet there are always a few moments in which, if we choose to be, we can be free.)

We are all so focused on shifting our goalposts that our goals become our very shackles. Life has started to resemble, in spirit, the infamous elephant story that many of us might have heard as children:

When a mahout starts to train a baby elephant, he ties its legs to a tree to restrain it from running away. After trying for a while, the baby elephant realizes that it doesn't have the power to free itself. Once the elephant gets older, the mahout stops shackling the elephant to the tree because he knows that for the mighty elephant, it will take less than a minute to uproot the tree. However, the elephant still doesn't run away because its mind has been conditioned to being shackled—to believing that it doesn't have the power to free itself.

The same way, we shackle ourselves to love, money, relationships, gluttony, and lust, and forget that all these are just some of the numerous components of a vast and beautiful life; and that real happiness lies in cherishing the now.

The day we realize, accept, and start living our lives this way, we will start to feel truly fulfilled. Our goals shouldn't become the shackles that withhold us from doing what we truly want to do.

There are three important beliefs to imbibe about the worth of the present moment:

The first is that you already have what you need. Make sure you make the best use of this resource.

The second is that wherever you are in life is where you are meant to be. Be present, physically and mentally.

And the third, and the most important, is that you are alive right now and capable of doing something in the present moment, in the now.

Change your 'I want that' to 'I have this'.
Change your 'I wish I were there' to 'I am happy I am here'.
Change your 'I will do it then' to 'I can do it now'.

Here's an exercise I now want you to do. Write down three situations in your life where your goals or priorities have become your very shackles. For example, maybe you are stuck in a job that you don't like, but you still stay due to the fear that you may not find anything better. Merely writing these down wouldn't help you get free from these shackles, but it is a start. Just like the elephant bound by a non-existent tether, your mind also gets stuck in a place where you don't know you are stuck. You need to be aware of what robs you of that happiness that you have been searching for so long.

1.

2.

3.

Cherishing the present moment is the first step to understanding that time is just another aspect of life. The next step lies in understanding how you can utilize time in a manner that best suits you so that you can focus your strengths toward achieving your purpose.

The Three Modes of Approaching Time

Having emphasized the importance of cherishing the present, let me now steer the chapter toward a concept about how different people approach time in different ways. We may have different perspectives, goals, and choices, but at the end of the day, we tend to act in one of three ways: as an implementer, a manager, or a leader.

The table below provides a fair idea of the distinction between the three.

Implementer	Manager	Leader
Builds	Facilitates	Inspires
Hardworking	Tactful	Visionary
Does things by himself	Decides how tasks will be done and then supervises the team	Builds a dream team and then communicates her vision to them
Pours his heart and soul into a job	Knows how to talk people into doing tasks	Inspires people and aligns them to her vision

Are you an implementer, a manager, or a leader? Or do you tend to act in different ways in different situations? Before we work on identifying your prominent role, let us understand more about these three roles.

Implementer

The advantage that an implementer has over a manager and a leader is that his creation isn't dependent on others. While it may take some time for him to get an idea to materialize, the product that he builds is his own and not easily replicable. He is proud of his product and can vouch for its quality. It is sometimes difficult for him to work in a team as he usually wants things to be done in a certain manner. His biggest challenge is efficient delegation. The best example of a person who is an implementer is Sachin Tendulkar. There was no match to his skills as a player, but he was never able to lead a team well.

Manager

The manager is your best bet among the three in terms of getting things done efficiently. A manager is usually a person who was an implementer earlier in his life. He knows how important an implementer is in a team and looks to build an efficient team to get his work done. A manager thrives on delegation. He aspires to be a leader, but he doesn't understand that he needs to shed his inhibitions to be able to get there. Examples of great managers can always be found around you. When you find someone who creates synergy between various elements in a workplace, while also trying to move on to the next step, you know you have an excellent manager at hand.

Leader

A leader is one of the most complicated and yet inspiring roles that one can play. A leader develops a vision and then hires managers to lead her vision. She may be the face of a brand or a company but never the one who does the work. She believes that her vision is a gift that she passes on to the world. The rise and fall of the leader depend on how her managers expand on her vision. A lot depends on the culture that the leader generates because one word of a leader becomes the truth for her team. A thriving culture coupled with a great vision can create invincible brands or companies. What Steve Jobs has done for Apple or what Elon Musk has done for Tesla perfectly explains how a leader-driven company can be highly successful.

Which role do you think you play at work?

If you think you have to be the CEO or part of top management to act like a leader, then think again. Leadership is not about what position you hold but how you act and deal with the people around you. The same holds true for the other two roles as well. It is all about the way you think and act. Even if you are part of senior management, but you like to get your hands dirty and end up doing more than what your role requires, then you are an implementer!

It is clear that the three roles are interdependent. When an implementer creates, he needs a manager to get his work in line with that of others, and when a leader wants to innovate and build, she needs a team of managers and implementers to convert her vision into reality.

Are you curious to see what kind of a person you are? Or maybe you already know. Let us do an exercise to see if you are right, shall we?

First, I want you to think about a typical day at work. Or if there's no such thing as 'typical' in your line of work, then consider any day in the last week or two that looked like a happening day at work for you.

Now, split that day into ten slots of an hour each. Think of the tasks you performed in each of these slots, how you responded to these tasks, and whether you acted as an implementer, a manager, or a leader.

You do not have to be in a job where you perform diverse kinds of tasks to do this exercise. Even if you have a rather monotonous job, this exercise will yield interesting results. Because I don't want you to think of just labelling the activity you did; I want you to think about how you went about your work and how you coordinated with others in the process.

To accurately classify yourself as an implementer, manager, or leader, make use of these cues:

You act as an **implementer** whenever you:
- are too focused on your own task.
- don't ask for help from the people around you.
- disagree with someone's idea even before completely listening to it.
- keep thinking of how you can speed up the work process.
- complete a task before anyone else doing a similar task.
- take over a task that someone else was doing because they were not doing it your way.
- believe in taking responsibility for your work.

You act as a **manager** whenever you:
- ask someone to collaborate with you so that you can get things done faster.
- delegate your work to someone else.
- call for a group meeting to brainstorm on a persistent issue.

- encourage people to share their ideas with you and the team.
- work alongside an implementer when they get stuck with a task.
- step down from your seat to do something menial just because you felt like it.
- are worried about your team's progress or future, along with your own.
- attend to reports, complaints, and suggestions from your subordinates.

You act as a **leader** whenever you:
- live in a world of vision.
- don't believe in supervising your team while they work.
- make your managers believe in your vision.
- choose to discuss plans and work rather than review the day's work.
- place complete faith in your team to carry your vision forward.
- dislike or avoid looking at reports on a daily basis.
- often end up daydreaming because that is where your best ideas come from.
- hold unrealistic demands and expect your team to fulfil them.

Coming back to the exercise, fill in the Time column based on your usual work timings, and against that, add the manner in which you worked during that time. Remember, you can pick any day in the last one or two weeks for this exercise. An example of a partially filled-in table is shown below.

Hour	Time	Acting as a	Feelings		
		Implementer/ Manager/Leader	Negative	Neutral	Positive
Hour 1	09:00 AM to 10:00 AM	Leader	●	●	●
Hour 2	10:00 AM to 11:00 AM	Leader	●	●	●
Hour 3	11:00 AM to 12:00 PM	Manager	●	●	●

An hour is a lot of time, and you may have done different things during an hour, but in my experience of doing this activity with a lot of people, I see that the one-hour time frame works best. Go on and do the exercise in the given table. (Ignore the last column for now. Instructions for it will be given in the next section.)

Hour	Time	Acting as a	Feelings		
		Implementer/ Manager/Leader	Negative	Neutral	Positive
Hour 1			●	●	●
Hour 2			●	●	●
Hour 3			●	●	●
Hour 4			●	●	●
Hour 5			●	●	●
Hour 6			●	●	●
Hour 7			●	●	●
Hour 8			●	●	●
Hour 9			●	●	●
Hour 10			●	●	●

Let us now understand the Feelings column. Once you have filled in details about how you acted during every hour of your workday, you need to think about how you felt during this time.

(You may have felt a lot of different emotions in an hour, but I want you to think of the dominant emotion.)

Starting with hour 1, depending on whether you felt positive, negative, or neutral performing a certain task, connect the corresponding dots. A simple way of doing this is depicted below.

These feelings have to be analysed not based on how others made you feel during the day, but based on how you felt while working as an implementer, manager, or leader. For example, at 10:00 a.m., your subordinate may have done some work that was not up to the standards you expected. You immediately tell him where he went wrong and ask him to report back to you within the next hour with the necessary corrections. Now, that hour may not have been the most productive for the company; however, this task that you carried out as a manager made you feel positive, that is, you enjoyed doing it.

Hour	Feelings		
	Negative	Neutral	Positive
Hour 3	•	•	•
Hour 4	•	•	•
Hour 5	•	•	•
Hour 6	•	•	•
Hour 7	•	•	•
Hour 8	•	•	•
Hour 9	•	•	•
Hour 10	•	•	•

In the chart, I have expanded on the Feelings column alone. During hour 4, my feelings went from being neutral to negative, where it stayed for the next two hours. In hour 4, one of the employees in my team came up to me with a problem about one of the machines that he was unable to fix. I tried calling up some people who could repair the machine for me, but they too failed to respond. Because there was an urgent shipment that had to happen that day, I had to go down to the shop floor and assist my team in solving the problem.

Basically, I shifted from being a leader to being a manager. For the next two hours, as I was focused on that work, I continued to feel impatient about how I was spending my time. I felt that I could have made better use of my time as a leader but I was stuck solving problems that someone else could have solved for me. Later during the day, when I got back to strategizing about the business, I felt much better, and my feelings shifted toward the positive end of the spectrum. Toward the end of the day, as I wrapped up my work and prepared my schedule for the next day, I went back to being at peace and in a neutral state of mind.

Switch Points

It is important to understand that one role isn't, generally, better or worse than another. What makes one person feel good could be frustrating for another. Just because I didn't like to go down and assist my team in repairing the machine doesn't mean someone else in my position wouldn't enjoy it too. What comes naturally for one is an uphill climb for another. Moreover, on some days, what is otherwise usually enjoyable to you can still turn out to feel cumbersome. Therefore, you need to understand that any of these three roles can lead to positive or negative emotions.

What is more important is to understand the pattern of switch points. A switch point is that hour or moment when your feelings change from one state to another, and usually correlates with the transition from one role to another.

Switch points give you an insight into what you most like doing and what you don't. Once you fill out this role and emotions chart for at least four days, you will be able to find a pattern in your switch points. Once you closely analyse this pattern, you will find the role that you are most comfortable taking on. Whenever you switch toward doing what you like, you will feel positive, which will give you a fair idea of who you are within: an implementer, a manager, or a leader.

Once you have understood the role that comes most naturally to you, you should compare it against your purpose. If your purpose is not aligned to your role, it may be difficult for you to work toward that purpose.

For example, let's say you want to bring about a revolutionary change in your field or industry. You are not going to be able to do this being an implementer. Similarly, if you are a natural leader, it will be difficult for you to thrive in a place where you mostly need to work alongside managers and implementers.

The next question that one may ponder is which is the best role among the three. Well, there's no one role that's the best for everyone. The best role for you depends on the kind of returns that you expect out of life (remember you read about financial, social, and emotional returns in chapter 4?) and what your approach to life is. There are different returns that each role will likely bring.

For example, you will find that being an implementer often provides a sense of peace and autonomy, but may not always lead to a high financial return. You may think me a fool to claim that Sachin Tendulkar, who I called an implementer, doesn't have a high amount of financial returns. But his skill as an implementer is unmatchable and works in his favour. This may happen to less than 0.1% of the people. As a rule of the thumb, when people don't easily have the power to collaborate, their returns will most likely be less than the returns of those who do. But the amount of emotional returns one may get as an implementer is usually higher because he is able to flow with life more easily and is grounded in himself and his activities.

Being a manager will let you build and derive power from others and may lead to average financial and social returns. Meanwhile, for those who thirst for a higher and far-reaching purpose in life and want to stop at nothing, being a leader is the way to go. We must remember though that being a ruthless leader will result in lower emotional returns.

There is no such thing as getting the best of everything. The balance between leaders, managers, and implementers has driven the world to becoming what it is today.

We have talked so much about how you can cherish the time you have and how you need to align your natural traits with your purpose. But there is one important tool that can help you become someone who makes time work for them.

If you think that that tool is 'time management,' then I suggest you read the name of this chapter again. To have the upper hand over time, you need to do something more powerful: shift and strengthen your focus.

Channelizing Time with Priorities

"All of us have twenty-four hours in a day."
"Bill Gates has the same twenty-four hours that you and I do."
"What we do with our time determines where we reach in life."
"There is no excuse we can give for not using the time available to us."
"After all, time is one resource that we can never get back."

There are endless quotes about time management, and to be frank, I hate most of them. All these quotes indirectly accuse people of not valuing their time. But is it our time that we don't value or is it our priorities?

As much as it is essential to utilize the hours in a day, is it so important to micromanage them? I believe that time is not the most important factor to what we achieve in a day. I know that a lot of "time management" and "avoid procrastination" experts will raise their eyebrows at this. But I repeat:

Time has little to do with what you wish to achieve.

One of Einstein's most popular theories is the theory of relativity. He was once quoted as having said: "When you sit with a nice girl for two hours, you think it is only a minute, but when you sit on a hot stove for a minute, you think it's two hours. That's relativity." Time is relative. It is our involvement in a certain activity that matters more.

In other words, when we intensely direct our energy at something, we will find a way to get it done, without actively thinking of managing the time for it. Have you not noticed this around you?

- When an otherwise lazy person decides to lose weight and get in shape, he suddenly starts waking up at 5 a.m. every day to go to the gym.
- A usually distracted person who hates the word 'meditation' suddenly starts practising it just because his loved one has taken to it.
- After a near-death experience, a chain smoker changes his ways and follows a healthy lifestyle.
- A brilliant student gets into a difficult relationship, and, suddenly, her grades start to drop.
- A teetotaller undergoes a bad experience, and starts casually drinking and betting, and before you know it, he is an alcohol addict and a compulsive gambler.

What does time have to do with any of this?

Some would say that the above-mentioned incidents took their course because of destiny more than an individual's choice or decision. Another assumption!

In all these examples, the intention, priorities, and choices influenced the outcome more than destiny or an excessive focus on time. Like I already said in Chapter 5, destiny may put you in difficult situations, but the choice you make is still up to you. There is never a point in life where you don't have a choice. Everything depends on how you define your priorities.

How you manage your priorities and align them with the returns you desire will determine the course of your life.

Read that again because the moment you internalize this, your life will change forever. You need to watch your priorities because they tend to become your patterns. You need to watch your patterns because they start becoming your limiting beliefs. You need to watch your limiting beliefs because they have the power to disempower you.

**The rise or fall of someone depends as much
on their beliefs as it does on their destiny.**

When people really want to do something, they will make time for it, and when they don't want to do something, they will find an endless list of excuses to not get it done.

One of the biggest excuses that people tend to use is: "I don't have the time to do it." You can keep playing the 'time' card, saying you don't have enough time to do something, but the moment you set your priorities right, you are free from the constraints of limited time simply because you will end up making time for what you badly want to do.

While you keep making the 'no time' excuse, there are others who will keep at the goal you desire to achieve, and they will reach there before you. Then you will go back to blaming your circumstances, your self-defeating beliefs, and your past, as explained in Chapter 5.

**It's not that we have too little time to do
the things we want to do, it's that we try to
do too many things in the time that we have.**

One last thing: let none of this pressurize you into thinking that you need to be the serious go-getter all the time. The good thing is when you align your priorities to your purpose, you don't have to work on it every single waking moment. Take a break when you want to, watch Netflix, get more than enough sleep, laze around, spend time with someone you love, be quirky, or try something for no solid reason. But while you do all of this, be aware. Be aware that beyond these breaks you take, there is a calling and purpose that awaits your action.

At the end of the day, what matters is you spend your time in a way that you best understand, in a way you are most comfortable with, and in a way that justifies your efforts. Simply put, you need to learn to choose your battles wisely. We will talk more about this in Chapter 10.

Chapter Summary

- We forget to cherish a goal/accomplishment because we have been taught to jump to the next goal as soon as we reach one.
- We are all so focused on shifting our goalposts that our goals become our very shackles.
- We tend to act in three ways or a combination of two in our life- as an implementer, a manager, or a leader.
- There is no such thing as getting the best of everything. The balance between leaders, managers, and implementers has driven the world to becoming what it is today.
- Time has very little to do with what you wish to achieve.
- How you manage your priorities and align them with the returns you desire will determine the course of your life.
- When you align your priorities with your purpose, things seem much simpler to accomplish.

CHAPTER

9

A Comfort Zone Is Never Comfortable!

**"SURVIVAL is about getting used to pain.
LIVING is about finding some meaning in the pain."**

Sagar Makwana

The Importance of Taking Chances

**Sometimes it's not the losing,
but the not trying that kills us.**

"But Aarav is so young, and . . . and I need you around, Sagar."

"I know that, Devangee. But this seems like too good an opportunity to miss!"

Devangee and I were discussing if I should join the Train the Trainer course offered by IATD (Indian Academy of Training and Development). I was just back from their introductory seminar, and I was quite sold. The issue though was that the course duration was four months and required me to spend all my Sundays in a class.

"I don't understand these things, but I am just worried that you will give me lesser time than you already do! You work twelve hours a day, six days a week, and now you want to do THIS on Sundays? How is that fair, Sagar?"

"But . . . Devangee . . . Fine, I will tell them that I can't join." I let out a sigh with my trademark puppy dog face.

"Sagar, please don't do this. You know I can't see you like this. But try to look at this from my point of view. I already feel that I don't get enough of your time."

After a long pause, I said, "You are right. Let me think this over. But I want you too to think about it. Assure me you will?"

She just nodded her head and didn't say anything further.

The next week was a tough one for me. I weighed the pros and cons of joining the course. I had a few intense discussions with

Devangee and even my dad. I have to be honest here: there were more cons than pros. But my gut was telling me to go for it.

Well, eventually, I did join the course and it turned out to be wonderful. The experience was completely different from anything I had had earlier. I was surrounded by the most heterogeneous crowd there could be—people from the age of 19 up until 76, of both genders and different backgrounds, and I made some wonderful friends among them. It was also here that I met Dr. Rajan (founder of IATD), who would eventually become one of my training mentors.

But the initial days of the course were anything but easy—it was extremely challenging to manage work, home, and the requirements of the course itself. I had to skip work to go to classes sometimes, apart from having to spend all my Sundays there. It didn't help either that there were some issues at work, and I wasn't there to solve them. My team was so used to my presence that they felt I was abandoning them.

Work pressures aside, Aarav was just a year old and was giving Devangee a hard time. What was more heart-breaking was that he was starting to forget my face. I was missing out on all his important milestones too. It was painful.

Devangee was handling it well at her end, but I could see the sadness in her eyes every time I told her I had to leave. And I could never leave without first answering her question, "When will you be back?"

"As soon as I can" was my usual fallback.

By the end of the first two weeks, I was regretting my decision to join the course. But I decided that I had to go on. There was no turning back now.

The weeks passed, and the course was soon nearing its end. It was time to give my final presentation of the course—an intense forty-minute speech on any topic of my choice, and I drove myself crazy preparing for it.

Interestingly, the day of the presentation also happened to be my birthday, thanks to Anjale, our course co-ordinator. (I shouldn't have pulled her leg so much through the course! I thought.)

As I began the speech, I felt a bit nervous, but slowly, I found my groove. As a part of my birthday surprise, Devangee came there along with Hiral and Reena (my monster-like sisters!). Finally, I got done with what I felt was one of the most exhilarating experiences of my life. I was surprised to see Dr. Rajan enter the class after my presentation. Much to my surprise, he said that he had been watching my presentation from his office on Facebook Live. The class ended with his encouraging feedback and a small cake-cutting ceremony.

Later that night, I sat on the sofa in my living room, replaying the events of the day, when Devangee came and sat beside me and looked me in the eye.

"Sagar, I want to talk to you about your presentation today," she began. I nodded my head slightly, nervously urging her to go on.

"Yesterday, when you were practising in front of me, your delivery seemed forced. I wasn't too impressed. I didn't say anything because I didn't want to put you down." She took a pause.

By now, my heart was in my mouth.

"You know what, Sagar? The last four months have been so difficult for us. I hope you can agree with me."

I just stared at her, wondering where this was going.

She continued. "And while you were presenting today in front of the audience, my mind kept thinking about all that I had to sacrifice for you: my sleep, my peace of mind, my time with you. Handling Aarav alone was such a big task by itself! I know I haven't complained much, but on some days, I felt you were being selfish."

I was dumbfounded. This wasn't what I was expecting. I mean, it was my birthday. Did she really have to speak all this now? I just wanted to tune out, and I put my head down.

She then held my hand, lifted my head slightly so that she could look into my eyes and said, "But today, when you were up on the stage, you were flawless. Your delivery, your subtle sense of humour, your interaction with the audience, everything seemed perfect. And I felt that these four months have been worth it; every sacrifice, just worth it. I have never ever been prouder of you, Sagar."

I stared at her for a few seconds. "Um, okay. Wait . . . What?" I gasped. "YOU!" I grinned, and we both started to laugh.

At that moment, I could feel an immense sense of pride. My mind went back to the day four months ago, when both of us were not sure about me doing this course. I was grateful that I went ahead and joined the course anyway. In the end, all that mattered was that the risk paid off.

This chapter is about harnessing the courage to step out of our comfort zone; about harnessing the courage to take risks. The more I think about it, the more I realize that this is a theme that holds enormous implications for all the major roadblocks and life-changing decisions of our lives.

In most situations—although one could argue that it applies to all situations—we have little clue of the outcome. Things could turn out well or badly. The results could be well beyond our expectations or turn out to be an utter disaster.

If I didn't do well in the course, I would have accepted that training wasn't my cup of tea. On the other hand, when I did do well, it made me realize that my calling did lie in coaching and that I was right in doing this course. What mattered here was not the result but the courage to explore. Only if you decide to try something new in your life and objectively observe the outcome, being prepared to face it either way, will you understand if your effort was worth it or if you should try something else the next time.

Most of us hesitate to take risks. We don't try to investigate if we will be good at something; if we should do something new that we have never tried before. And this indecisiveness eventually kills us from within. You may exceed your expectations or fail. But you will know it only if you take a step forward. And how you handle the success or failure that arrives is what defines you as a human being.

Think about all those decisions in your life that you feel you should have gone ahead with—taking up that new job that was way out of your comfort zone, asking out that close friend who could have turned out to be more than just a friend, taking a risk as an entrepreneur that you weren't sure would pay off, patching up with a closed one whose bond you really valued, opening up to your loved ones about how much you value them before it is too late. The amount of risk that each person will be willing to take could be different, but I don't know of anyone who has regretted trying something that they wanted to do.

I am not saying that everything will work out just fine if you take that step. But not taking the step is sometimes even more difficult to digest. The course that I took got over in January 2020; within two months, the COVID pandemic hit the world. Had I not done the course back then, I would have lost the opportunity to do it altogether because, as of January 2022, they have not been able to recreate that course. Life has its ways of making us realize how to connect the dots. I would suggest you look closely at all these signs.

I have come to realize that most people postpone or never take decisions because they fear getting out of their comfort zone. But the comfort zone is not a good place to be in because you are constantly undermining what you can achieve as a human being. Allow me to narrate a small story around this.

Arthur Berry was a charming man who loved only the finest things life had to offer. During the Roaring '20s, he was a master thief who stole from only the wealthiest people. Berry was eventually caught and spent the next eighteen years in prison. After serving his sentence, he moved to a small town in New England, where he led a quiet life.

Some years later, word got out who he was, and his identity attracted a horde of reporters who came to interview the notorious thief. One reporter asked him, "Do you remember who it was that you stole the most from?"

Berry replied, "The person that I stole the most from was Arthur Berry. I could have contributed to society. I could have been a teacher. I could have been a businessman. I could have done anything worthwhile, but instead, I spent two-thirds of my adult life in prison. I have spent a lifetime robbing myself."

I have come to realize some important things from this story.

Everyone who does not know their art is a thief.

Every person is a thief who does not use his full potential.

In conclusion, he is a thief who does not identify his talent and use it for exemplary work.

The Seven Steps to Stepping Out of the Comfort Zone

"Real change is difficult at the beginning, but gorgeous at the end. Change begins the moment you get the courage and step outside your comfort zone."

Roy T. Bennett

How does one get out of their comfort zone and take more risks? This is a tricky question because each of our comfort zones is different. And what risk means to each of us is also different. But fortunately, the broad stages that we all must go through in this journey remains the same.

These are seven steps that we must all inevitably cross before we reach our destination, but as you will soon see, the term 'destination' itself is subjective in this system. I am going to narrate these steps along with the story of one of my close friends, Suresh Kumar.

Suresh is the youngest among three brothers. When he was a child, there was constant financial crunch at his home, and he had to deal with the burden mentally and physically. His mother's biggest aspiration for his life was that he become a bus conductor one day. And even though Suresh didn't believe in limiting himself, there were enough people around him to tell him to do just that.

After he finished his schooling, Suresh wasn't allowed to pursue a college degree for two reasons: his family was not financially stable, and his mother did not believe education would help him in the future. Suresh, therefore, had to take a break and took up some petty jobs. He soon realized that this was not how he wanted his life to turn out and slowly started to save up to enrol for a bachelor's degree in law. But he eventually settled for a degree in commerce via distance education so that he could continue working to be able to provide for his family. Suresh finally came close to finishing his B.Com. in 1999. Unfortunately, he ended up having an arrear in a subject that he struggled to clear for the next two years, and this just squashed his dreams of getting any worthy job.

At this point, not just his mother, but the whole family saw no hope for him. Suresh was desperate, and he tried working as an office boy, a clerk, and later took up a job as a door-to-door salesman. A year or two passed, and he started doing well for himself. Looking at his sales skills, his brother decided to set up a shop that Suresh could handle. Three years passed, but the business didn't pick up as well as had been expected. His brother then began to blame Suresh for all the loss, and Suresh felt that he was right in doing so.

Then came the pivotal moment in his life. In 2005, he decided that enough was enough, and with the money that he had saved, he went back to getting a law degree. Three years later, he became a lawyer at the age of 29. He got a job offer at two different places and decided to work in one of them. His life turned around, and he was soon earning well enough. It was also around this time that he got married.

You may think this is a good enough end to the story, but Suresh's story doesn't end here. In fact, the best part has just begun. Even though things stated to work in his favour, Suresh had a feeling that he wasn't living up to his potential at the job. He felt that he was getting into a comfort zone and wanted to get out of it. He approached his wife and told her his predicament. His wife, his biggest strength in life, asked him to do what he felt was right. This was all he needed to hear. He quit his stable, well-paying job to start his own practice—his vision was to become a trademark, copyrights, and patent lawyer.

Did this risk that Suresh took pay off? We will see. Using our seven-step framework, let us chart Suresh's journey from the moment he decided to step out of his comfort zone of a stable job.

Having listened to numerous people recount their biggest risks and most challenging life experiences, I have been able to zero in on the seven stages that one transitions through when they decide to step outside their comfort zone. Each of us will encounter these seven phases. Some of us, however, will give up in the middle and never reach the last step. Knowledge of these seven steps and knowing that we are not alone in our struggles—that this is something everyone faces—will help us overcome our challenges better.

1. Self-Doubt
2. Denial
3. The Initial Steps
4. The Setback
5. Courage
6. Finding Meaning in Pain
7. The Sweet Taste of Success and Accepting the New Norm

Self-Doubt

Every aspiration is accompanied by one simple feeling: self-doubt. It doesn't matter whether you are an experienced professional or someone trying something different for the first time. Self-doubt arises in everyone's mind—even if they do not explicitly acknowledge it. When you are in this stage, there are a few questions that will constantly ring in your head:

Do I have what it takes to do this?
Do I really need to do this?

The last time I tried doing something different, it went horribly wrong.
What if it happens again?
Will everyone around me be able to accept this change?
What do I even get out of this?

This is how our brains have been wired. The fight or flight instinct usually makes us choose flight as our first option. We tend to run away from novelty. It is sometimes okay to embrace this self-doubt because it prevents us from taking some highly irrational decisions. But more often than not, it squashes our dreams even before they have had a chance.

Self-doubt will persist until you take the first step out of your comfort zone. It is certainly not helpful that other people will also point out your past failures and pull you down. But despite all this, when you move forward, you will slowly find your path and the courage to pursue it.

When Suresh decided to start his own firm, he first approached friends and family to ask if it was a good idea. As expected, he got a lot of negativity and discouragement in return; he was reminded of what had happened earlier when he tried to start a business. Not one to go down without a fight, Suresh went and asked a few other lawyers if they would like to partner with him to start a firm. Of the fifteen people he approached, only two showed some interest in what he wanted to do. With that minimal support, he decided to take another plunge into the world of entrepreneurship. But in his mind, it was not easy to shake off the lingering impact of his past failures.

Denial

After self-doubt comes a stage that is, in some ways, worse than self-doubt: denial. You start to think that having stepped outside the comfort zone was unnecessary in the first place. You start finding reasons to not proceed further. The worrying part is that many of these arguments will be valid.

"People will choose unhappiness over uncertainty."

Tim Ferris, The 4-hour work week

At this stage, you will start to believe that you are fine exactly where you are and that you don't need to push harder. You fear that the uncertain roads that lie ahead will compromise your security and happiness.

During this stage, the people who can influence you will matter a lot because only they will have the power to shake you out of this denial.

Once Suresh resigned from his job, he wanted to set up his law firm with two other partners who had earlier shown interest in his idea. He had the expertise and expected the support of the other two for investment and client acquisition. But to his shock, both backed out at the last minute, and Suresh had no option but to start the business alone. Suddenly, it hit him that he was now all alone and had little idea of what to do.

Suresh was now down on his knees; he felt that maybe he was wrong and that he should just go back to a job. He went to his wife and told her what he felt. At that time, she was making money by providing home tuition to kids. She told him that he shouldn't give up on his dream and that she will handle the daily expenses. She encouraged Suresh to go ahead and start his business. In 2011, Suresh rented a small office space of 50 sq. ft. with his wife's hard-earned money and began his company under the name 'Unimarks Legal Solutions'.

The Initial Steps

After some convincing, your mind will let you go on your journey. The first steps are the hardest, but the first accomplishments are also the sweetest. Your first order, your first chapter, your first pitch, your first working code, your first milestone—these will make you realize that you were right in taking this path. Further, now that you have broken the main initial barriers of doubt and denial, you will also come up with several ideas and be filled with the enthusiasm to try different things in your endeavour.

Suresh's wish was to establish expertise as an IPR lawyer in trademarks and patents. However, realizing that this wouldn't give him a lot of earnings, he also took up odd cases from the municipal courts to the high court. Over the next three years, when he could only get about a hundred clients for trademark cases, he realized he needed to change something. That's when he decided to hire someone for marketing, and this turned things around for him. In the next one year, he added fifty more clients to his firm; now it felt like things were on track. But, alas, it didn't stay that way for long.

The Setback

Sometime around the start of 2015, Suresh found some of his clients acting strange: They were pulling out of deals at the last minute, and his lead conversion rate had started to fall. When he looked further into this, he found out that the person whom he had hired for marketing was funnelling clients to his own firm. When confronted, the guy simply shrugged and said he didn't want to work with Suresh any longer. He quit, but not before taking over a hundred clients (about sixty-six percent of the clientele) with him. This was a huge slap in the face for Suresh.

We often assume that our growth curve will be linear. We believe that once we take off, it will only get easier. But things will start to go wrong. We will hit unexpected hurdles and lose our way. This is because the learning curve is filled with a series of bends and deflections.

We start off well and assume that it will all work out, but there are certain implications and possibilities that we don't consider. The gap between the straight line that is our expectation and the curve that is reality is what I call "the valley of disappointment".

The setback stage is different from the self-doubt stage because now we know better how to work around our disappointments and use our learnings to get better at what we do. We have faced difficulties before and come this far, so we wouldn't be prone to give up easily. That said, for us to bounce back stronger, we need one crucial ingredient: courage.

Courage

> **"I learned that courage was not the absence of fear, but the triumph over it. The brave man is not he who does not feel afraid, but he who conquers that fear."**
>
> *Nelson Mandela*

Fear is an integral part of every journey that we undertake. In fact, it is fear itself that propels us forward. The fear of failure, the fear of missing out, the fear of not proving ourselves, the fear of not earning enough, the fear of not achieving success. When this fear doesn't stop us from getting ahead and achieving our goals, then it is a sign of courage and determination.

For Suresh, it took a lot of courage to build his business back after losing over 65% of his clients. But this time, it was different.

This time, he knew what he had to do when he fell. He persevered and just kept doing what he had been doing. He formed another team and focused on his strengths. Gradually, he started gaining traction, and within the next three years, he expanded his client list to a whopping four thousand clients.

Finding Meaning in Pain

Once you cross the major setbacks, it becomes easier. Not because there are no more hurdles, but because you get used to facing them. I remember a story from an inspiring talk given in 2019 by Mr. Raju Venkatraman, the CEO of Medall Diagnostics Pvt. Ltd.

Being a serial entrepreneur, he was also a mentor to a lot of people who ventured in start-ups. He was planning to mentor a couple who had founded a start-up and ran their venture with a lot of zest and rigour. They had been working in the corporate sector for more than ten years and were excited to embark upon this journey of entrepreneurship.

Mr. Raju recalled an interesting conversation that he had had with them. One day, during a discussion, the lady had asked him a question.

"Sir, I have heard from a lot of people that the entrepreneurship journey is difficult. Is it true?"

Mr. Raju had replied, "Yes ma'am, the first three years are especially difficult. You need to gear yourself up for some tough times."

To this, she had asked, "Oh, is that so? What happens after three years then?"

"Oh, after that . . . after that, you get used to it," Mr. Raju had responded, and as he recounted this to us, we roared with laughter.

The journey of entrepreneurship is much like life. There will be pain, failure, setbacks, and let-downs. But among all these will also be joy, success, encouragement, and a lot of cheer! A small set of people understand that it is this pain that has made them realize who they are and what they are meant to do in life. These are the people who are in real pursuit of purpose and happiness.

In 2021, Suresh inaugurated a 4700 sq. ft. office for his firm, Unimarks; he currently employs more than forty people and has branches in Tirupur, Bangalore, Ahmedabad, and Kolkata. At the time of this book being written, his company has filed more than 18,000 trademarks. Today, Unimarks files about four percent of all the trademarks filed in South India. Suresh is also an investor in another firm, Pearlpick Ventures Pvt. Ltd., that offers end-to-end business solutions to entrepreneurs. His wife is the CEO and a major shareholder of this firm.

Suresh continues to face challenges, but it doesn't stop him from doing what he does. When he sees that he is able to support so many people's livelihoods and inspire the people around him through whatever he does, he continues to work despite the pain. He has found meaning in his pain, and this pain is the driver in his life.

No one has ever been proud of what they have achieved by leading a life devoid of pain. With pain comes learning, with learning comes meaning, and with meaning comes purpose. Always remember:

SURVIVAL is about getting used to pain.
LIVING is about finding some meaning in the pain.

The Sweet Taste of Success and Accepting the New Norm

The last stage of the process is enjoying the sweet taste of success and accepting the new norm. But here's the caveat: this isn't the final stage. There is no final stage, simply because there is no end to growth.

Our journey uphill from an initial comfort zone is accompanied by a lot of pain and effort; it takes a lot of time too. But once we reach a mark of victory, we are quick to settle down here and make it the new comfort zone. One important reason for this is that we like it here. We own the place like it's our own and rightly so: it took a lot of pain and effort to get here, and we have all the right to feel grateful and proud; to want to take the liberty to enjoy our time here.

But sometimes, we mistakenly start to believe that everything is just going to be easy from here. Well, it will be, but not for long, simply because we aren't built to wallow in comfort zones. Howsoever you look at it, life is short, and before you know it, your best years will be behind you. When you step outside your comfort zone into new challenges, new explorations, and new learning, you truly begin to utilize this gift of life. You do need to bathe in the glory of having come thus far, but you also need to slowly move ahead. Be grateful for where you have reached but also have the courage to go even further.

**"Intellectual growth should commence
at birth and cease only at death."**

Albert Einstein

When he started off in a 50 sq. ft. office space in 2011, Suresh didn't envision getting to a 4700 sq. ft. office in 2021. Truly, this must be his time to sit back and enjoy the fruits of his hard work. And yet, after having done all that he has, Suresh realizes that he is in yet another comfort zone. When I was done interviewing him for this chapter, he showed me his vision board for the next five years. Apart from leading a healthy lifestyle and a fulfilled life with his family, Suresh's vision is to employ at least 1000 employees in his organization, and to achieve this, he knows that he will have to come out of his comfort zone over and over again.

After talking to him about his journey, I realized one important thing: that the journey we undertake in our life can never be devoid of effort, right until our last breath. The biggest example I can cite for this is Dr. APJ Abdul Kalam. He was 83 when he passed away. But he didn't die in a hospital bed, unable to exercise his intellect or his capabilities. He died of cardiac arrest late in the evening while he was giving a lecture at one of the premier institutes in India.

His contribution to India and to the world is unquantifiable and unquestionable. But his desire to inspire, to ensure that his knowledge and experience will continue to live on made him not stop until his last breath.

He could have stopped a long time ago and let go. But his commitment, his energy—that could not be taken away. I am not asking you to compare yourself to Dr. Kalam. But I would like all of you to think about your moment of death. Morose though it sounds, try to think of that moment. It could be tomorrow, the next week, the next month, or decades later. When that moment comes, would you be happy for all that you did in your life or will you die not having done what you wished to do a long time ago?

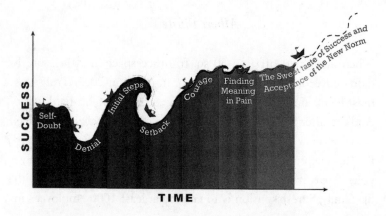

Chapter Summary

- Sometimes it's not the losing but the not trying that kills us.
- The first step to getting out of your comfort zone is to take a risk.
- Being in a comfort zone is never good because you are constantly undermining what you can achieve as a human being.
- Real change is difficult at the beginning, but gorgeous at the end.
- There are seven steps to getting out of your comfort zone: Self-Doubt, Denial, The Initial Steps, The Setback, Courage, Finding Meaning in Pain, The Sweet Taste of Success, and Accepting the New Norm.
- Stepping out of your comfort zone helps you achieve a fulfilled life.

10

Connect the Dots, Make It a Circle

**"You are not a drop in the ocean.
You are the entire ocean in a drop."**

Rumi

As you may well be aware by now, numerous personal anecdotes feature on the pages of this book. I believe that our own life stories are the best fodder we have to reflect and draw lessons from—not Internet quotations, not bestselling memoirs, not business case studies, but the incidents that we lived, laughed, or fought our way through. Throughout the book, I have shared with you snippets from my life that have taught me important lessons in their own subtle ways. I hope you could relate to them or remember similar memorable incidents from your own life after reading them.

In a way, it is safe to say that this book and its exercises have all been a subtle nudge toward preparing you for a brand-new beginning. And when I say a 'beginning,' I intend it to be one that is devoid of all assumptions that you may have had earlier. I know I keep saying this again and again, but you need to understand that your mind has mostly likely fooled you more often than you know, and your subconscious mapping is sometimes too difficult to get rid of. That is why we started this book with breaking down all the existing assumptions, using the techniques of First Principles Thinking, as outlined in chapter 1.

After discarding those assumptions that have held us back for so long, we set about to find our What and our Why. In chapter 2, we learned that our purpose and priorities should always be defined and explored with a sense of Why. Do remember that the Why we have in our mind today may no longer exist tomorrow because we will grow, we will mature, and our ideas about an ideal life will change.

Chapter 3 taught us to become aware of our core strengths among money, relationships, ambition, and time. Our portfolio of strengths will bring its own unique returns: financial, social, or emotional. We learned about these returns in chapter 4. More importantly, we now know how to be aware if our returns and strengths support our purpose or not. When they are misaligned, then we need to either work on our strengths or change our priorities. What's important is to be aware. Once this awareness sets in, along with conviction about our goals, then nothing can stop us—not our circumstances, not our self-defeating beliefs, and not our past, all of which was explained in chapter 5.

And we do have friends along the way—friends within our own subconscious mind—who constantly strive to support us and guide us in the right direction. These are the three inner voices: the achiever, the believer, and the comforter, which chapter 6 described. Meanwhile, it is important to cultivate strong relationships outside, too. The power of this synergy is strengthened when we have the right set of people around us, as described in Chapter 7.

Chapter 8 made us aware of how we prefer to function with respect to time and how we can direct our focus toward priorities to challenge time itself. But even if we direct our focus on our dreams, there will be doubt. There will be denial. There will be complacency and a tendency to settle down into a comfort zone. How we can overcome all this was outlined in chapter 9. We understand the importance of marching on in life with the single aim of never settling down in a comfort zone, not until the day we die.

The Power of NOW!

I hope that when you finally get on a path true to your inner self, all the concepts that I have laid down in this book will guide you in the right direction. But before I let you go, let me share with you two powerful parting thoughts. The first is one of my favourite Satty stories.

Satty is a dear college friend of mine. It takes less than two minutes for anyone to figure out that Satty is a huge cricket fan. He has loved, enjoyed, and followed cricket for as long as he can remember. His father too is a cricket fanatic, and this definitely helped Satty's case. If there was a match on television, Satty's mother knew that she couldn't get any work done from the father-son duo. He has grown up watching matches right from the Sachin era to the now Kohli era. He is such a huge fan of Kohli's captaincy that he immediately became an RCB fan when Kohli was named captain of the team. But this story is set in a period when he was much younger and entering a dramatic phase of his cricket-worshipping life.

The year was 2003. Satty was thirteen years old. Sachin Tendulkar had not yet been named the God of cricket, but everyone revered him nonetheless.

New Zealand cricket team was touring India, and they were playing a match in Chennai, Satty's hometown. During those days, getting tickets to watch a match in the stadium was a big deal, and they were expensive too. A kind uncle gifted Satty's dad two tickets so that he could take Satty to watch the match live. This was the first time that Satty was going to see a match in a stadium and he was overjoyed.

Being the child that he was, he demanded that he see the ticket a day before the match; he snatched it from his father's hand and he went to his room, dancing all the way. He wanted to sleep with the ticket in his hand! He was so excited that he couldn't even sleep, and kept feeling the ticket in his hand the entire night.

It was a day/night match and Satty had planned the whole day ahead. The match was supposed to start at 2:30 p.m. His dad had to give an important presentation at work that morning, after which they were supposed to leave by 12:00 p.m. as per the plan. Since they lived just half an hour away from the stadium, Satty figured that they could reach there well before the match would begin. He had everything planned out:

Step 1: Paint his face with the tricolour as soon as they reached the stadium.

Step 2: Stake out all the cameras in and around his seat.

Step 3: Hold up a Sachin banner with an obnoxious quote to get noticed by the cameramen.

Step 4: Shout "India! India!!" every time the camera panned on him.

He had thought of everything!

The day finally dawned. Satty sat up on his bed, after a long night of waiting, with the most excited face his father had ever seen on him. That morning, his father asked Satty to give him the ticket so that he could keep it safely, but Satty was adamant that he will take care of it by himself. He saw his dad off to work and anxiously waited for him to return.

Alas, life being at its cruel self that day, his father got stuck at work and came late. Time to switch to plan B, Satty thought. He decided to forego the painting-the-face part of the plan so that he could reach before the toss. There was enough time for that, he thought. They left as soon as his dad came in, and he was happy to finally get his plan moving.

But Murphy's law wasn't very kind to Satty that day. They reached halfway, when suddenly their scooter got a flat tire, and they had to get that fixed first. He saw his father pull the scooter to the nearest puncture repair shop, and while the scooter was getting fixed, the repair guy started to make small talk. It was all getting on Satty's nerves, really. Get the job done faster please, he thought.

Over the radio that was in the shop, it was announced that India had won the toss and chosen to bat first. Great! Satty thought. Now he had missed the toss too, and there was just half an hour before the match would start. Satty nervously looked at his father, while the mechanic muttered something under his breath. But his father's face was expressionless. Satty was boiling with frustration!

His only plan now was to be there before the first ball was bowled. They were less than ten minutes away from the stadium. It seemed plausible. Finally, the tyre was fixed and they drove on.

Since they were late, they had to park far away from the stadium, but, well, at least they were finally there! Only five minutes were left for the first ball, and Satty couldn't wait to get in now. His father asked him to keep all his belongings in the glove compartment of the scooter to avoid losing anything.

While they neared the stadium, Satty could hear the people inside screaming, "SACHIN, SACHIN!!" It felt surreal. The match was about to begin. Satty was trying to hurry as fast as he could on his little legs! His father was equally animated! They reached the gates of the stadium, and the usher asked for the tickets. His dad gave his and signalled Satty to take out his.

And that's when Satty remembered! Along with his other belongings, he had also left the ticket in the glove compartment! Oh God! he thought. His dreams came crashing down. He begged his dad to let him go in alone, while his dad could collect the tickets from the scooter. But fearing Satty's safety, his father didn't budge.

Satty kept cursing himself, "How could I be so stupid? Dammit!" By the time they finally managed to get inside, Sachin had already put twenty-one runs on the board, and the match was taking an interesting turn because Sehwag had just gotten out.

Satty was pissed. He was mad at his dad's boss for making him work late, at his destiny for the punctured tyre, and finally at himself for forgetting the ticket in the scooter! He didn't want to watch the match any further. His dad obviously wasn't happy with this attitude and scolded Satty for his lousy behaviour.

When Satty recounted this incident to me, several years later, he spoke of it as though it had happened just the previous day. Now, I understand why. He missed the beginning of the match—the first live match of his life—and somehow that was such a huge deal. He was even okay missing the toss, but his mind wasn't ready to miss the start of the match, so much so that he didn't want to watch the rest of the match. Seems silly, isn't it? But think about it. Don't we all have this bias toward wanting a fresh start?

Does watching a movie after missing its first fifteen minutes feel the same as watching it from the beginning? Would you be okay to have the memories of the first eighteen years of your life erased in return for an obscene sum of money? Wouldn't it irk you to not be able to relive the childhood innocence, the fun of your teenage years, and the life lessons you learned in college?

Do you know why adults often wish to return to childhood? It's simply because there are so many 'firsts' in that phase: the first cycle, the first set of crackers, the first Holi, the first cricket match, the first speech, the first failure, the first crush, the first victory, the first day at the hostel, the first love, the first break-up. So many moments of exhilaration that just can't be replaced.

We love beginnings because they are loaded with the promise of effort, adventure, and learning. Try to imagine the excitement that arises when you do something you are passionate about, the anxiety before performing something for the first time, and the fear of facing a new challenge. There's a high point you reach, and then it's usually downhill from there until the next 'first'.

The good news is that this sense of exhilaration needn't be confined to childhood. You can recreate the same sense of youthfulness and excitement every time you initiate and embark on a new journey, whether to learn a new skill, begin a project, create a website, write a book, or even just start a new habit. Anytime you venture to do something new, you will feel a sense of excitement that you can't shake off, and you will feel as if you have been born again. Nothing can beat that feeling of trying something for the first time. And that is why when there's nothing new for you to do—when you stop experimenting, when you stop failing before winning—you start losing interest in life.

Again, here's a secret: you don't even have to wait to get on a project to experience this high point. All you need to do is start looking at each day as a fresh start.

Drawing inspiration from the famous phrase, "KAL HO NA HO" (who has seen the new tomorrow? What if there's none?), I say this:

Life gives another day to a man/woman who wants it and takes away from the one who regrets it.

Imagine if you can get as excited about the start of every day as you would when you start a new assignment or a task. Would you feel as low as you usually do? Probably not. When you learn to harness the power of your mind, you can easily learn to treat each day this way.

One way to do this is to repeat a silent affirmation. It doesn't have to be a prayer to God. You also don't have to thank anyone for the life that you live. Rather, I want you to say something similar to what I said earlier in Chapter 5:

We are nothing but who we are in the reality of this fleeting moment.

Yes, this moment is all that matters—your attitude, effort, and commitment right now. Just be yourself and accept the moment as is. Acknowledge and accept that you are at peace. This moment then becomes your zero point, and anything and everything you do from now is a gain. When you start doing this every day, you will be gifted with the power of NOW. And that gift is as priceless as life itself.

This is exactly how I felt when I decided to write this book. Being in the moment gave me a sense of self-belief, a sense of understanding, a sense of satisfaction, and most importantly, a sense of power that eventually enabled me to begin this journey and cherish it every day. And I hope that as you are about to finish this book, you hold that same belief in yourself, have the same clarity, and feel as satisfied and empowered as I did on that day.

I hope that you continue your journey without any assumptions, treating every day as a new one. Because you matter. Yes, you do. And if you don't believe it yet, then the next and the final section of this book is for you.

Nothing, Something, and Everything

**"We are all going to die, and for me,
that's what makes life worth living."**

From the book UNLEARN

It was a rainy Sunday afternoon in Mumbai. There's something about Mumbai rains that makes one rather philosophical. I was having a chat with my cousins, Neha and Sakshi. I knew both these teenage girls were going through some troubles.

We started talking about life, and one thing led to another. I asked Neha about her studies, her vision for life, and so on. She casually remarked, "What's the point? We are all just leading meaningless lives."

I wasn't comfortable with this statement, and I asked her to elaborate. She said she believed that none of us or anything we do mattered in the larger scheme of things and that it's all just an inevitable, useless, slow march toward death.

It seemed to me that she felt that her life didn't mean anything and whatever she had done so far and what she planned to do meant little to her. I was certainly taken aback. I looked at Sakshi, and she had a look of agreement that showed that she too believed what Neha had said.

I just sat back on the sofa and looked them in the eye. I tried explaining to them that whatever they were thinking may sound deep, but there is certainly another side to it. I started my usual talks about how we were all meant to fulfil some purpose in life. But they didn't budge.

They protested, quoting Alexander the Great, for support. During one of his speeches, he had said, "When you bury me, please leave my hands hanging out of the grave so that the world can see that the greatest man in the world didn't take anything with him and his hands were empty when he died." Their argument was that if even Alexander the Great didn't have anything to live for, then what are we, the petty peasants, living for. We are NOTHING.

Nothing. That's when it struck me. They were looking at life as a destination, whereas they should have been looking at it as a journey.

I took a deep breath. "What's nothing?" I asked them.

"What?" they stared back.

"What is nothing? Define it," I persisted.

"Um, nothing is nothing, duh! Not any single thing. It has no meaning," they replied, shrugging.

I then asked them how there could exist a word in the English language without any meaning.

After some thought, they said, "The absence of something is nothing."

I continued, "Excellent! Can you then tell me the meaning of 'something'?

Neha thought for a few seconds and then said, "Well, something is . . ."

Sakshi interrupted to finish Neha's sentence: "Something!"

I laughed. Sakshi again: "Something can by anything—this table, this chair, this sofa!"

I paused and gave them a serious look. "Okay, then what are you? Are you also 'something'?"

Neha quickly retorted, "Of course, yes . . . but . . ."

I stopped her right there. "Wait, wait, wait. Before you start running in a different direction, answer this: what is 'everything'?"

This time, they didn't hesitate: "A collection of things, or every single something is everything."

I clapped. They looked at each other, bemused.

I asked, "So can there be everything if there is *one* something missing?"

Neha replied, "Of course not! Everything means *everything*. Even a single thing can't be missed out!"

"Well, that's where your answer lies," I remarked, with a smile.

Both just stared at me blankly. I went on to explain, "You say that 'everything' is incomplete even if it misses one thing. Well, then you have to agree that this world is incomplete without you, right?"

To this, they had a defeated, but also intrigued, look on their face.

I continued, "On the canvas of the universe, you may be just a line or a stroke of brush, but if you aren't there, that canvas stays incomplete. After you, maybe that stroke will be painted over by someone else, but as long as you are there, you add meaning to it."

On that day, they hopefully realized an important lesson.

I am not here to say that you will become the richest or smartest or most powerful person in the world. I am not here to say that your opinion will someday be heard all over the world. But I can assure you of one thing: As long as you are a line on the canvas or even just a dot, you matter. And you must try to play that role to perfection. Because if you don't consider yourself important, the whole of creation loses its value. And any creation, however small or big, is meant to be something.

NOTHING is a waste. Even a marshland can hold a lotus, even the cowardly show courage in times of despair, even the infidel believes in himself, even the most desperate people in the world cling to hope. It is through this hope that they eventually, after a long, hard struggle, build their legacy; that they do justice to their potential and contribute something to the lives of others too, making all the pain worth it. I hope you carry on, too, with this attitude and forge your legacy. The world awaits you.

Chapter Summary

- Our own life experiences teach more than the books, people, or the internet.

- Anytime you venture to do something new, you will feel a sense of excitement that you can't shake off, and you will feel as if you have been born again.

- When you imagine every start of the day with the excitement of a new beginning, you will always accomplish more than you wanted to.

- We are nothing but who we are in the reality of this fleeting moment.

- If you don't consider yourself important, the whole of creation loses its value. And any creation, however small or big, is meant to be something.

Acknowledgements

The first person I want to thank here is me (give me a moment before you call me a narcissist). Over the journey of this book, if there's one thing I have realized, it is that you can't write a book on self-awareness without having been a self-critic and battling self-doubt. Hence, I thank the self-critic and the self-doubting Sagar, for going through all those phases in life, for constantly learning from them, and for never giving up.

Thank you, Devangee. You are the biggest pillar of strength I have. Words aren't enough to tell you how much I appreciate your presence in my life. You are the reason I feel like I am alive. You are the reason I believe I can serve my purpose in this world; simply because the unshakeable faith you have in me and my abilities make me feel invincible. Thank you for pulling me out of the darkness of my own arrogance, my ego and filling it with the light of your love. Just know that everything I do has a part of your reflection in it.

I am indebted to Maa and my sister Hetal. Thank you for being who you are and for letting me be who I am. Thank you for teaching me invaluable lessons of gratitude, patience, emotions, and love.

Hiral, your illustrations have portrayed my thoughts in the most effective manner possible. I am proud of you, sis, for what you have achieved in your life. Thank you for never leaving my side.

Thank you, Sinduja and Mansi, for being supportive and critical of my work so that I could get better every day. Without you, this book wouldn't have been in the shape that it is today.

Thank you, my publishers, Gaurav Sabharwal and Shantanu Duttagupta, for helping me take this book to the world. Garima, you are a wonderful editor and I want to thank you for your guidance and positivity.

Thanks, Suhail, (The Book Bakers) for having the first faith in my writing and my concepts.

Finally, thank you, Universe, for guiding me in my path, surrounding me with friends who always have my back, and filling my life with wonderful experiences. I want to let you know, this is just the start.

S agar Makwana is an entrepreneur by profession, and a
speaker and coach by passion.

After graduating with a degree in engineering, Sagar,
who turned 33 this year, worked with Tata Motors for a
while, before beginning his own entrepreneurial journey. He
has been successfully running his automobile components
manufacturing business for over eight years now. His company,
JyoAsh Engineers, which he named after his mother and
father, began with just four employees and now employs over
eighty people.

Sagar's active participation in the world of coaching began
after acquiring his Master's Diploma in Training from IATD
Chennai in 2019. Since then, he has passionately involved
himself in his journey to bring about change by spreading
positivity. He even launched his own signature course "Let's
Love Living" in 2020 that has impacted more than three
hundred people so far. The program is designed around a set

of activities that helps participants to tap into the power of their subconscious mind.

A firm believer in the power of introspection and self-awareness, Sagar likes to make people uncomfortable with thought-provoking questions. His coaching sessions are usually vibrant, interactive, and intuitive.

When Sagar realized that one could assess life and its priorities in a systematic manner, he decided to launch a new training program and also write a book on this method. He wanted to step away from the usual show-problem-give-solution approach that most self-help books propose.

Be You. Now! is the result of this journey and will help people discover what works best for them. Sagar's experience as a corporate employee, entrepreneur, and now a trainer, speaker, and mentor has provided fodder for many of the book's concepts that will strongly resonate with readers.

Sagar believes that life is tough, and that it is meant to be so. However, it is the way people deal with it that defines their journey. He also believes that coupled with a passion to eat, pray, and love, life's musings are best enjoyed when shared with others.

Connect with him

Email: sagarmakwana@gmail.com
Instagram: @oceanofsynergy
Linkedin: https://www.linkedin.com/in/sagarmakwana/
Facebook: https://www.facebook.com/SagarAMakwana/